Home Office Research Study 219

Evaluation of close supervision centres

Emma Clare and Keith Bottomley
assisted by Adrian Grounds, Christopher J Hammond,
Alison Liebling and Caecilia Taylor

Centre For Criminology and Criminal Justice, University of Hull and
Institute of Criminology, University of Cambridge

*"The views expressed in this report are those of the authors, not necessarily
those of the Home Office (nor do they reflect Government policy)."*

Home Office Research, Development and Statistics Directorate
January 2001

Home Office Research Studies

The Home Office Research Studies are reports on research undertaken by or on behalf of the Home Office. They cover the range of subjects for which the Home Secretary has responsibility. Titles in the series are listed at the back of this report (copies are available from the address on the back cover). Other publications produced by the Research, Development and Statistics Directorate include Research Findings, the Research Bulletin, Statistical Bulletins and Statistical Papers.

The Research, Development and Statistics Directorate

RDS is part of the Home Office. The Home Office's purpose is to build a safe, just and tolerant society in which the rights and responsibilities of individuals, families and communities are properly balanced and the protection and security of the public are maintained.

RDS is also a part of the Government Statistical Service (GSS). One of the GSS aims is to inform Parliament and the citizen about the state of the nation and provide a window on the work and performance of government, allowing the impact of government policies and actions to be assessed.

Therefore -

Research Development and Statistics Directorate exists to improve policy making, decision taking and practice in support of the Home Office purpose and aims, to provide the public and Parliament with information necessary for informed debate and to publish information for future use.

First published 2001

Application for reproduction should be made to the Communications and Development Unit, Room 201, Home Office, 50 Queen Anne's Gate, London SW1H 9AT.

© Crown copyright 2000   ISBN   1 84082 592 8

ISSN   0072 6435

Foreword

The Prison Service's system of Close Supervision Centres (CSCs), for the management of disruptive prisoners, was introduced in February 1998 to replace the former network of special units established in the late 1980s.

The Prison Service commissioned Professor Keith Bottomley of Hull University to undertake an independent two year assessment of the new CSC system and the results of his evaluation are set out in this study. Professor Bottomley led a multi-disciplinary research team comprising criminologists with extensive experience of prison research, forensic psychiatrists, and an economist as consultant for the cost-effectiveness analysis .

The researchers argue that the CSCs' central underlying principle of prisoner 'progression', through a variety of incentives and earned privileges, is seriously flawed with respect to the management of these particular prisoners and that their management should be based on a set of rather different operational principles and processes. The key elements should include:

- a comprehensive assessment process which includes substantial and integrated clinical input from forensic psychiatric services and others, in order to identify personality disorder and mental illness, and to assess risk.

- the establishment of differential regimes with safe and humane conditions in which the minimum threshold should be standards and conditions that at least equate to those found in dispersal segregation units.

- the long-term containment of a small number of high risk prisoners whom it would be unsafe to return to normal location, even when they have spent many years in the CSC system and have progressed to the top level.

A great deal of work is now being done by Prison Service to take this agenda forward - including developing the work being done in dispersal segregation units to manage the kind of disruptive prisoners who might otherwise be candidates for the CSC system.

Chris Lewis
Head of Offenders and Corrections Unit
Research Development and Statistics Directorate

i

Acknowledgements

To undertake this extensive evaluation required the cooperation of a large number of people, not just in the Close Supervision Centres themselves, but in dispersal prisons, at Newbold Revel and at Prison Service Headquarters as well – in fact too many people to enumerate separately.

However, we would firstly like to thank Dr Adrian Grounds and Dr Caecilia Taylor for all the work they did on the psychiatric evaluation of the centres and to our economist colleague Christopher L Hammond who was our analyst and consultant for the cost-effectiveness part of the study.

Particular thanks are due to Dr Alison Liebling for putting her extensive prisons research experience at the disposal of the team and for setting out the findings of the research within the context of prisoners' incentives and earned privileges. Thanks are also due to Professor Richard Sparks who acted as academic consultant to the project and who provided his thoughts on how research should be taken forward in this area.

Within the Home Office, the authors would like to thank John Ditchfield (Research Development and Statistics Directorate) and Diana Luchford (Directorate of High Security Prisons) for helping to manage and supervise the research and Phil Wheatley, Brodie Clark and Peter Atherton who, at different times during the research, were responsible for the centres and who all supported and encouraged our evaluation.

Finally we would like to give our special thanks to the governors, staff and prisoners of the Close Supervision Centres at Woodhill and Durham themselves – without whose interest and cooperation the evaluation would obviously have been impossible.

Emma Clare
Keith Bottomley

The authors

Keith Bottomley is Professor of Criminology at Hull University.

Emma Clare is Research Fellow at the Institute of Criminology, University College, Dublin.

Dr Adrian Grounds is University Lecturer in Forensic Psychiatry at the Institute of Criminology, Cambridge.

Dr Caecilia Taylor is consultant forensic psychiatrist at Kneesworth House Hospital, Bassingbourn cum Kneesworth, Royston, Herts.

Dr Alison Liebling is Senior Research Associate, Institute of Criminology, Cambridge.

Richard Sparks is Professor of Criminology at Keele University, North Staffordhire.

Chris Hammond is lecturer in economics at the University of Hull.

Contents

Executive summary

1. Aims of CSC system and methods of study

The Prison Service's system of Close Supervision Centres (CSCs), for the management of disruptive prisoners, was introduced in February 1998 to replace the former network of special units established in the late 1980s, following the recommendations of the Control Review Committee (1984), and generally known as CRC units. The CSCs were also intended to take prisoners previously placed on the Continuous Assessment Scheme (CAS).

Statement of purpose

The original 'Statement of Purpose' in the Operating Standards for Close Supervision Centres described their role as follows:

> Close Supervision Centres will operate as part of a national management strategy which aims to secure the return of problematic or disruptive prisoners to a settled and acceptable pattern of institutional behaviour.
>
> 2. The functions of Close Supervision Centres will be

> i)   to remove the most seriously disruptive prisoners from mainstream dispersal or training prisons.

> ii)   to contain highly dangerous or disruptive individuals in small highly supervised units with safety for staff and prisoners.

> iii)   to provide the opportunity for individuals to address their anti-social disruptive behaviour in a controlled environment.

> iv)   to stabilise behaviour and prepare for a return to the mainstream with minimum disruption.

A fifth function was added to the CSC Operating Standards in April 1999:

> v)   the long term containment of those who continue to pose a serious threat to the safety of staff and prisoners.

Methods of study

The main elements of the research fieldwork and data collection during the two year evaluation (June 1998 – June 2000) were as follows:

(i)   Observation of the day-to-day running of the CSCs: extended periods of observation were carried out, mainly by Emma Clare, and totalled 96 days.

(ii) Interviews with prisoners and staff in each Centre (including governor grades and specialists) were carried out by EC (assisted by KB), and totalled 35 CSC prisoners and 63 staff at Woodhill, Hull and Durham.

(iii) Psychiatric interviews: the consultant forensic psychiatrists (AG and CT) carried out psychiatric assessment interviews (using structured diagnostic schedules) with a total of 23 prisoners, including 14 at Woodhill and nine at Durham; these constituted approximately three-quarters of those resident in the CSCs at the time.

(iv) Documentary material relating to CSC prisoners: inc. CSC referral forms; prisoners' CSC files and main prison records; incident reporting system; and the local inmate data system (LIDS).

(v)   Management accounting data for the cost effectiveness analysis were provided by the finance sections at HMP Durham and HMP Woodhill, and by Prison Service Headquarters.

(vi) Staff training and in-house evaluation: Emma Clare attended several CSC staff training events and in-house evaluation meetings.

(vii) CSC Selection Committee and Monitoring Group: all meetings of the CSC Selection Committee (February 1998 – April 2000) were attended by EC, as well as Unit Managers' meetings; meetings of the CSC Monitoring Group were also attended by one or more members of the research team.

(viii) Dispersal prisons and High Control Cells (HCCs): two series of visits were made (by KB and EC) to each dispersal prison, in June 1999 and April/May 2000, to review their experience of the CSC system.

(ix) Data on order and control in the dispersal estate: selected data were extracted from the Order and Control matrix on serious incidents in dispersals for the period before and after the opening of the CSCs.

We first summarise the findings of our evaluation, and then consider how far the official functions of the CSCs appear to have been fulfilled to date. Finally we identify key issues for the future development of the CSC system.

2. Selection of prisoners and population trends

Prisoner selection

In its first two years of operation, the CSC system managed a total of 51 prisoners. Over half of these prisoners had previously spent time on the Continuous Assessment Scheme (CAS), which was formally closed in February 1999.

Seven of the 38 prisoners on the CAS scheme in February 1998 were not transferred to CSCs but managed in some other way. However, apart from one prisoner who subsequently assaulted an officer, virtually all those ex-CAS prisoners appeared to have settled down on normal location within dispersal or other long-term prisons.

Forty-six prisoners were referred to the CSC Selection Committee in the first two years, of whom 22 were selected for the CSCs. Three-quarters of those turned down for the CSC system continued to be held within the dispersal system without causing any further serious trouble.

All but perhaps one of the prisoners selected for the CSC system during this period fitted one or more of the official CSC selection criteria, having extensive records of serious violence and disruptive behaviour both inside and outside prison.

Population trends

Thirty-six prisoners were managed at Woodhill during its second year, with the average population being 26. Of these, 11 prisoners spent their time being moved between A wing and D wing – with seven of them also being moved out to High Control Cells for periods totalling 4–6 months each. Eight prisoners refused to cooperate with the system throughout most of the first two years.

During the second year, 16 prisoners in Woodhill could be said to have been attempting fairly consistently to progress. Eight prisoners progressed from Woodhill to the Activity Intervention Centre in Durham G wing; a further three progressed to Durham I wing.

Durham I wing managed an average of eight prisoners for most of its first two years, with its lowest number in the second year being six. Four prisoners spent the whole of the second year located on I wing.

Durham G wing opened in May 1999. The build up of prisoner numbers was quite well managed – reaching seven by April 2000. Two prisoners progressed from G wing to normal location in the mainstream, with several other prisoners likely to be deselected in the near future. Two prisoners were returned to Woodhill due to further disruptive behaviour.

Three of the prisoners in G wing seemed likely to need long-term containment in the CSC system, due to the high risk they continued to pose to the safety of staff and/or prisoners, and despite having complied with the system sufficiently to progress to G wing.

3.   Regime provision in the CSCs

Woodhill – C wing
In the first year virtually no constructive activities had been provided for prisoners on the Programmes Intervention Centre (C wing) at Woodhill. The situation improved slightly in the second year, but there was still a high level of boredom and inactivity on C wing throughout most of the period. Some of the professional and resource problems relating to the provision of appropriate group work on C wing were eventually resolved, so that two Enhanced Thinking Skills (ETS) courses were provided in 1999.

Woodhill – B wing
The role of the Structured Regime Centre (B wing) at Woodhill was to provide an assessment of the prisoners at the point of entry to the CSC system, that should then inform the subsequent decisions about their location and progress. Although a version of the Dispersal Induction Assessment (DIA) was piloted on B wing, the development of an appropriate assessment tool for CSC prisoners should be given priority.

The main problem on B wing throughout the second year continued to be the struggle that staff faced simply in carrying out the basic daily routines of unlocking, feeding, showering and exercising prisoners, which meant that there was little time or energy left for more constructive activities and meaningful staff-prisoner interaction.

Woodhill – A wing

Prisoners' perceptions of the regime on the Restricted Regime Centre (A wing) were very negative throughout the two year period. There were very few signs of the wing being able to fulfil its intended role in the CSC progressive system, in which staff were supposed to encourage prisoners to move up to B wing. Although the Operating Standards were revised to ensure that the physical conditions in A wing were comparable with those in dispersal segregation units, this had little effect on prisoners' perception of the almost wholly punitive impact of the Restricted Regime Centre.

Woodhill – D wing

D wing did not fulfil its original role as the segregation unit for the CSC wings, but had to cope with persistently confrontational behaviour from a group of prisoners who refused to cooperate with the CSC system and were engaged in acts of concerted indiscipline, dirty protests and violence/threats of violence against staff. Whilst fully appreciating the dangers to which staff were exposed on D wing, the resultant conditions and regime on D wing were in our view unacceptable.

Durham – I wing

The role of Durham I wing was to provide a therapeutic regime with psychological and psychiatric support, particularly for those prisoners whose disruptive behaviour was linked to their psychiatric and mental health.

One of the main characteristics of I wing throughout the first two years was the high level of staff-prisoner interaction. There was, however, a significant reduction in the psychological input to the Centre in the second year, following the resignation of the experienced senior psychologist in June 1999. No full-time replacement was found until the end of the year and this had a considerable effect on the amount of specialist individual and group work that was done with prisoners.

Durham – G wing

G wing was handicapped, at the start, by the lack of adequate preparation for the transfer of the Activity Intervention Centre from Hull A wing, which closed earlier than anticipated. As a result, and due to the general shortage of psychological and psychiatric resources at Durham, it was unable to provide the individual counselling and programmes that were planned. Although a part-time clinical psychologist was later appointed and undertook some individual work with two prisoners in G wing, there was a failure to deliver the regime stipulated in Operational Standards.

4.   Management and staffing issues

Staff turnover and retention

All the CSCs experienced considerable changes in their management structures and senior managers during the first two years. In addition, particularly at Woodhill, there was a significant turnover of uniformed staff which increased the pressures on existing staff to carry out their essential duties. It was difficult to recruit enough suitable volunteers to work in the Woodhill CSCs.

There were fewer problems of staff retention and recruitment at Durham, largely because of the more positive profile that work in the CSCs continued to enjoy there. However, several staff were coming to the end of their initial tour of duty on I wing, where the nature of the staff-prisoner interaction made it vital to retain as much continuity as possible and to recruit officers with a strong commitment to the ethos of the wing.

Staff morale and effectiveness

A number of broader issues relating to the local management of the Centres at Durham and Woodhill also affected staff morale and effectiveness. For example, the CSCs at Woodhill did not enjoy the same degree of operational autonomy that was apparent at Durham and which contributed significantly to the development of the positive staff culture and 'camaraderie' that was a distinctive feature of I and G wings.

At Woodhill, in contrast, the early events on A and D wings affected all the CSC staff to some degree, including those working in B and C wings. These exceptional and largely unanticipated circumstances highlighted the problems inherent in the physical design and staffing arrangements of the Woodhill CSCs.

One of the results was the emergence of a fairly clear split within the Woodhill CSCs at the beginning of the second year between A and D wings, focusing on control and containment, and B and C wings working towards progressing the prisoners through the CSC system. This hindered the development of an integrated system based on the original progressive aims of the CSCs.

Local autonomy issues

Because of the high political and media profile of the CSCs, it was understandable that they should receive a great deal of attention from senior Prison Service management. As a result, many management decisions about CSC matters, that arguably should have been handled by local management, were 'pushed up' to a higher level. The net effect was an undermining of the confidence of staff at different levels in their ability to do the jobs that their rank would normally entail.

The role of psychiatry and psychology

The psychiatric assessment of the CSC prisoners revealed the extent and seriousness of mental disorder among this population, in particular their high rates of mental illness and its co-occurrence with personality disorder. The implications of these findings are serious in relation to the provision of clinical services and in relation to those prisoners who have been kept in solitary confinement in D wing for extended periods.

The emergent picture of prevalent mental disorder amongst the CSC prisoners was particularly disturbing in view of the lack of adequate psychiatric support for the CSC system from the outset and the relatively limited input that forensic psychiatrists and psychologists have had in the assessment process on B wing. These assessments have been seriously handicapped by the refusal of many prisoners to have anything to do with the psychologists; and most provide little psychological or historical understanding of the prisoners' personalities and emotional lives.

There was a lack of relevant knowledge about the personalities, background and motivation of the CSC prisoners at virtually every stage in the system, starting at the point of referral and selection, through that of initial assessment and continuing into the Centres themselves where individual and group work with prisoners was intended to address their disruptive behaviour and enable them to progress through the system.

5. Prisoner progression and the effects of the CSCs on prisoner behaviour

Despite the development of a containment role for the CSCs, the notion of 'progression' has remained central to the system. Therefore, the number of prisoners who progress through the system and are returned to normal location remains one of the key bench-marks for measuring the success of the CSC system as a whole. On this criterion, the system cannot be said to have enjoyed a great deal of success in its first two years.

Between February 1998 and May 2000, 12 prisoners were transferred out of CSCs, either to Special Hospitals (4) or normal location in the mainstream (8). Two of the prisoners transferred to Special Hospitals were subsequently returned to the prison system (because of renewed violence) and re-referred to the CSCs. Of the prisoners returned to normal location, only four have so far been able to settle without any recurrence of their disruptive behaviour. In summary, therefore, two-thirds of the prisoners who progressed from the CSC system in its first 28 months failed to survive their departure from the Centres.

Comparing the disruptiveness of prisoners whilst in the Centres with their pattern of behaviour prior to their admission to the CSCs, we concluded that 30 prisoners showed a reduced level of disruptive behaviour in the CSCs, compared with their record outside the system, whereas six prisoners showed an increased level of assaultive behaviour in the CSCs. The remaining ten prisoners, for whom we had information, showed little change in either direction.

Eight prisoners refused to cooperate with the system from the outset and embarked upon a persistent campaign of confrontation and challenge, involving dirty protests, violence and/or threats of violence against staff, as well as litigation against the system. In the cases of some of these prisoners, their behaviour deteriorated dramatically following their transfer to the CSC, and therefore the overall effect of the CSCs on these prisoners has been negative.

6.   Impact of the CSC system on order and control in dispersal prisons

There is no comprehensive data set for measuring accurately the levels of disruptive behaviour in the dispersal estate before and after February 1998; nor, if such data were available, is it possible to attribute any such change directly or solely to the influence of the CSCs. So many other management initiatives and changes have been introduced into the long-term prison system during the past five years, that any or all of these could have contributed to the improved situation in dispersals. Nevertheless, there are a number of indicators that suggest that the CSCs may have made a contribution to reducing the level of disruptive behaviour and facilitating the management of order in dispersals.

Data from the Prison Service's incident recording system and 'Order and Control' matrix, for the three years preceding and the two years following the introduction of the CSCs, confirm that there was an overall reduction in serious incidents in dispersal prisons in 1998 and 1999. There were reductions in hostage taking, concerted acts of indiscipline and reported assaults on prisoners and staff.

Our research visits to all the dispersal prisons during the past two years confirmed that not only had the CSC system taken out of circulation a group of very disruptive prisoners, but provided relief from the task of coping with the 'merry-go-round' of CAS prisoners.

The number of prisoners being held in dispersal segregation units on a long-term basis has significantly decreased in the past two or three years, which has allowed them to develop a range of promising initiatives for the handling of any difficult behaviour by their own prisoners – thereby hopefully preventing them from becoming future candidates for referral to the CSCs.

7.   Cost effectiveness

The critical factor in the consideration of the cost effectiveness of the CSC system is the assessment of the benefits it has generated. Unfortunately, in designing the system apparently little consideration was given to the nature of the potential benefits or how they might be realised. Consequently, there is no solid foundation on which to base an evaluation. Further complexity has been added to this situation, as the anticipated outcomes of the system proved elusive and operational objectives were changed.

Although the fieldwork revealed several aspects of the management of disruptive prisoners which have been improved, either directly or indirectly as a consequence of the CSCs, many of the findings are subjective and some more speculative. To attempt to place a value on such effects would require an even greater degree of speculation and a high risk of misrepresentation.

The benefits of the CSC system may become more apparent when the effect on the pattern of prisoner behaviour can be assessed from a longer term perspective. However, given the severe limitations of the data and the difficulty in isolating the effects of the CSCs from other changes, it is unlikely that a formal benefit evaluation of this episode will be feasible.

Although the CSC units are not identifiable cost centres in Prison Service accounting data, by focusing the management of disruptive prisoners in a small number of Centres the costs are more readily identifiable. Our central estimate of the cost per annum of a place in the CSC system implies that the incremental cost against the benchmark of normal accommodation in a dispersal prison is of the order of £55k per year. However, the full economic cost may have been substantially greater, though this is partly accounted for by the transitional conditions under which the system has operated throughout the period.

Although retrospective analysis at some future date might clarify the benefits of the CSCs and enable a formal evaluation of at least some aspects of their effect, our tentative conclusion is that they are unlikely to be judged cost effective in purely accounting terms. If cost effectiveness is to be used in assessing the future development in the management of highly disruptive prisoners or other groups where special provision is required, more consideration must be given to the identification, monitoring and systematic recording of outcomes and effect.

8.   Incentives and progression in the CSC system

At the heart of the CSC system, as conceived by the Spurr Report, was the notion of a system of staged Centres that offered incentives for cooperative behaviour, with progressively more privileges at each level. It was intended to have a dual containment and progressive function, and was designed with some of the most intractable prisoners in mind.

In practice, however, the Structured Regime in B wing at Woodhill was seen by prisoners as offering an unacceptable lowering of material privileges; and from the outset the Restricted Regime in A wing (and also D wing) were regarded as entirely punitive and the target of bitter contempt from a group of prisoners unwilling to cooperate with the new system in any way.

The initial emphasis on 'progression' meant that little attention had been paid to the 'regressive' option or downward spiral, so that CSC staff were unprepared for the degree and nature of the refusal of certain prisoners to cooperate or 'progress'.

Early experience of the CSC system confirmed the inappropriateness for these prisoners of the 'rational choice' and 'instrumental reasoning' models of behaviour underlying the IEP framework. The perceived relevance to them of conventional material privileges was seriously misjudged.

A further drawback of the 'progressive' model of the CSC system was that both compliance and risk reduction were necessary for full progression and return to the mainstream. Problems and frustrations were created by and for those prisoners who complied but were too high a risk for returning to normal location. Compliance was no guarantee that the underlying causes of their disruptive behaviour had been addressed and the level of risk thereby reduced.

9.   Integration with the long-term prison system

The general level of knowledge about the functioning of the CSC system among staff in dispersal prisons was still quite limited, especially regarding the work of the Centres at Durham. However, the increase in staff exchanges and visits had begun to improve the situation.

The use of High Control Cells in dispersals provided an important point of contact with the CSC system; new standards and guidelines had been introduced to ensure greater consistency of provision. There is a need for greater communication between the CSCs and dispersals regarding the treatment and behaviour of CSC prisoners in High Control Cells.

As relatively few prisoners had progresssed from the CSCs and returned to normal location in dispersal prisons during the first two years, there was little experience and few procedures in place for the re-entry and reintegration of prisoners. However, formal arrangements have now been drawn up for 'transition plans' to ensure closer liaison between the CSCs and the receiving prison.

10.   The functions and achievements of the CSC system

We shall now briefly review the extent to which the five official functions of the CSC system appear to have been fulfilled to date.

(i)   The removal of the most seriously disruptive prisoners from mainstream prisons

The 51 prisoners managed by the CSC system in its first two years were clearly prisoners who had caused serious disruption in dispersals; over half of them had been in the CAS system immediately prior to transfer to the CSCs and many of the rest were being held in dispersal segregation units.

The CSC selection process appears to have been quite successful in identifying those who posed a continuing threat of disruption, as the vast majority of those not selected subsequently appear to have settled down in normal location.

Following the establishment of the CSC system in 1998, and a reduction in the number being held long-term in dispersal segregation units, dispersal prisons have been in a better position to manage successfully any disruptive behaviour that may occur, thereby hopefully preventing the emergence of a new generation of persistently disruptive prisoners.

(ii)   The safe containment of those prisoners in small highly supervised units

There appears to have been a reduction in the disruptive behaviour of a majority of CSC prisoners following transfer into the system; however, violence and serious threats to the safety of staff came from a significant minority of prisoners in Woodhill who refused to cooperate with the system and adopted a persistently confrontational stance.

The behaviour of this group of prisoners (located in A and D wings at Woodhill) also affected staff working in B and C wings, who were not able to feel safe from actual or threatened violence.

Similarly, in the more open conditions of Durham I and G wings (and before that in Hull A wing), prisoners expressed real concerns about their safety, in such close proximity to some notorious and manifestly unpredictable prisoners.

Even D wing was not perceived by staff or prisoners as a safe environment, but as one that posed real threats to the personal safety of staff and prisoners, as well as to the mental health of those held in solitary confinement there for any length of time.

(iii)   The provision of opportunities to address anti-social disruptive behaviour

The structured regimes of Durham I and G wings allowed positive interaction to take place between staff and prisoners. Although problems were experienced in the second year relating to specialist psychological and psychiatric support, a staff-prisoner culture continued to flourish (especially in I wing) which was conducive to bringing about change in prisoners.

In contrast, B and C wings at Woodhill largely failed to achieve this objective, partly because of the lack of an effective assessment system to indicate the individual and group work that needed to be done with these prisoners, and partly because of a failure to recognise (in many cases) that tackling their mental health needs was an essential prerequisite to helping them address their anti-social behaviour.

(iv)   To stabilise prisoner behaviour and prepare them for a safe return to the mainstream

There is evidence that the behaviour of perhaps one third of CSC prisoners may have been 'stabilised' to some extent during their time in the Centres. This was not the case with the group of prisoners who refused to cooperate with the system nor for many of those who failed to progress satisfactorily through the system.

In the first two years, 12 prisoners (less than a quarter of the total) progressed through the CSC system and were transferred out, either to Special Hospitals or to normal location in the mainstream prison system. Of these, two prisoners were subsequently returned to prison from the Special Hospitals and reselected for the CSCs, with only four prisoners appearing to have settled on normal location. Thus, the number of cases of successful reintegration and return to the mainstream so far seems low, in the context of the official overall objective of progression.

There were a few cases where the CSC system identified mentally ill prisoners and managed to transfer them to special hospitals, but there were often serious delays and problems in the working relations between the CSCs and the mental health services. Examples of men returned to the prison system from special hospitals suggests that the high-security hospitals are currently failing in their role of managing certain dangerous mentally disordered prisoners.

(v)   Long-term containment of those who continue to pose a serious threat to the safety of staff and prisoners

This fifth function for the CSCs was added to the Operating Standards in April 1999, because of the emergence of two particular groups of prisoners, namely (i) those whose aggressive non-compliance undermined the central notion of progression, and (ii) those whose assessed risk was too great for them to be returned to the mainstream – despite having met the other criteria for 'progression'. The CSC system so far has failed to deal adequately with either of these two groups of prisoners.

The regimes in A and D wings at Woodhill were not appropriate for the long-term control and containment role which they were required to fulfil in the first two years of the CSC system, with the group of non-cooperating prisoners who were shuttled to and fro between A and D wings, plus occasional 56 day 'cooling off' periods in a High Control Cell in the dispersal estate.

Similarly, alternative provision is necessary for the small number of prisoners who may meet the criteria for progression through the system to Durham G or I wings, but are too dangerous and of unpredictably high risk to be returned to normal location. To keep them indefinitely on G wing would not only be potentially dangerous for other prisoners and staff but would affect the dynamics of a wing that is intended as a re-entry unit for preparing prisoners to return to the mainstream.

11. Key issues for the future development of the CSC system

Several key issues need to be addressed in developing an effective and humane strategy for the management of disruptive prisoners. Any new developments should be firmly grounded in the increasing body of knowledge relating to the personalities and mental health of these prisoners, and the strategies they adopt for coping with the stresses of imprisonment.

Underlying assumptions and principles

We believe that the central underlying principle of prisoner 'progression', through a variety of incentives and earned privileges, is seriously flawed with respect to the management of these prisoners – particularly if there is an unreasonably austere and restrictive starting point.

The events of the last two and a half years have shown that the behaviour of the prisoners admitted to the CSC system is far more complex than was generally recognised at the outset. The 'privileges' on offer were not perceived by many prisoners as of relevance or value to their individual situations. As a result many failed to respond to the incentives for progression but instead challenged the system's basic principles and the fairness of its procedures and practices.

At the root of the problem, in our view, is a lack of proper understanding and appreciation of the background histories and damaging experiences which these prisoners bring with them into the CSC system. These personal histories and experiences have frequently been associated with the prison system and in many cases are linked to and/or have contributed to disturbed mental states. Accordingly, the progressive principle is unrealistic.

The management of disruptive prisoners should, therefore, be based on a set of rather different operational principles and processes. The key elements should include (i) a comprehensive assessment process; (ii) the establishment of differential regimes, with safe and humane conditions; and (iii) the long-term containment of high-risk prisoners.

(i) Assessment and case management

Because disruptive prisoners are a very heterogeneous group, each with their own individual histories, emotions and attitudes, a comprehensive assessment is a vital first stage in their proper management. This assessment must include substantial and integrated clinical input from forensic psychiatric services and others, in order to identify personality disorder and mental illness, and to assess risk.

To assist this process, ways must be found of encouraging and enabling CSC prisoners to engage with the psychologists and other specialists, who are in a position to help them address the underlying causes of their behaviour.

The psychological assessment (incorporating appropriate risk assessment instruments) would provide the basis for the subsequent management of the prisoner. To achieve this, there needs to be an urgent review of the psychological and psychiatric resources available to the CSC system, to enable them to implement the individual management programme for each prisoner. Successful implementation will require close working relationships with basic grade and supervisory staff in each Centre, as well as with education and probation staff, and liaison with the special hospitals and outside agencies.

(ii)   Differential regimes

Because of the progressive system's serious limitations, when applied to these kinds of prisoners, a more appropriate set of operating principles and practices needs to be established. The minimum threshold should be standards and conditions that equate to or are better than those found in dispersal segregation units. These should obtain in the induction/assessment wing, where prisoners would normally expect to stay for a relatively short time until decisions have been taken about their future management.

The other wings at Woodhill and Durham should then provide a non-hierarchical range of regimes, matched to the control requirements and development needs of individual prisoners, and to be used with maximum flexibility. The standards and conditions in these wings should be comparable with those found on normal location in dispersal prisons.

Prisoners whose behaviour or attitudes on reception suggest that they are unlikely to cooperate with the system should be held initially (but for only a short period) in the segregation unit at Woodhill. If subsequent attempts fail to persuade them to want to work with the system, they should be returned to the dispersal system – possibly to a High Control Cell. Alternatively, there may be a case for the establishment of a dedicated unit for these prisoners, outside the CSC system, until such time as they feel able to 'sign-up' to the new aims and objectives of the CSCs.

Careful thought needs to be given to the management and staffing of the Centres in Durham and Woodhill. Wherever possible, each Centre should have its own staff complement to provide the continuity and mixture of experience/skills conducive to good staff-prisoner relationships and regime delivery. Each should be encouraged to develop its own sense of identity and distinctive role within an integrated system.

There is a strong case for the appointment of a full-time Director of CSCs, accountable to the Director of High Security Prisons. This would recognise the importance and demanding nature of the management of this group of prisoners, and relieve the High Security Director of some of the more routine operational decisions relating to CSCs.

(iii) Long-term containment of high-risk prisoners

There will always be a small number of disruptive prisoners whom it would be unsafe to return to normal location, even when they have spent many years in the CSC system. In a system based on the principle of progression, these prisoners have shown that they can progress through the system by satisfying the normal criteria. However, they then find themselves at the top level but still presenting too high a risk for safe return to the mainstream.

The problem has been recognised by the Prison Service, and proposals are under discussion about the nature and location of a special long-term containment unit for this group of prisoners. Removing the progressive rationale for the CSC system may help to resolve some of the problems, as it would allow more flexible movement of prisoners between Centres.

Similarly, the abolition of the present framework of incentives and privileges for CSC prisoners would open up the discussion about the appropriate living conditions for these long-term containment cases. Consideration should be given to providing for the special long-term containment of these prisoners in the dispersal system, outside the CSCs.

(iv) Future prospects for the prevention of disruptive behaviour

We have been impressed by the innovative work being done in many segregation units to manage disruptive prisoners who might otherwise be candidates for the CSC system. It seems vital that dispersal prisons should be encouraged and properly resourced to develop this kind of 'preventive' work.

Steps should be taken to improve communications between the CSCs and the dispersal system. This will not only help them in being better prepared to receive prisoners back from the CSC system but also help them to develop a sense of shared ownership and responsibility for the behaviour of prisoners in the system as a whole.

Finally, resources need to be made available for the systematic collection, monitoring and analysis of all information and data flows related to the management of disruptive prisoners. This should be used both for management purposes and for ongoing research into the nature and causes of severely disruptive behaviour. In this way it will be possible to build up a long-term knowledge base concerning difficult prisoners and their appropriate management.

1.

Introduction: terms of reference and methods of study

The Prison Service's new system of Close Supervision Centres (CSCs) was introduced in February 1998, to replace the former network of special units established in the late 1980s, following the recommendations of the Control Review Committee (1984), and generally known as CRC units. The CSCs were also intended to take prisoners previously placed on the Continuous Assessment Scheme (CAS), which was to be phased out at the earliest opportunity (for further details of the recent background to the management of disruptive prisoners, see Appendix 1).

Organisation of the CSC system

The CSC system currently consists of five Centres, of which three are located in HM Prison Woodhill and two in HM Prison Durham. Four of the five Centres form the core of this progressive system: the Structured Regime Centre (B wing, Woodhill), the Programmes Intervention Centre (C wing, Woodhill), the Restricted Regime Centre (A wing, Woodhill) and the Activity Intervention Centre (G wing, Durham), which was formerly located in A wing, Hull Prison (February 1998 – February 1999). I wing (Durham) has the more specialised role of managing prisoners with a history of highly disturbed behaviour and as such has a more self-contained role within the CSC system.

The Structured Regime Centre (B wing, Woodhill) serves as the assessment wing. The regime on this wing is intended to offer prisoners some opportunity to participate in constructive activities and personal development activities. Prisoners are allowed limited time out of cell for cleaning duties, exercise, interviews with psychologists and personal officers and also a period of association with up to three other prisoners.

The Programmes Intervention Centre (C wing, Woodhill) is intended to offer a challenging environment for prisoners, with their individual problems being addressed through structured activities, with a minimum of 20 hours of constructive activity per week.

The Restricted Regime Centre (A wing, Woodhill) is for prisoners whose behaviour is so disruptive that strict conditions of segregation are necessary to protect staff and prisoners. Prisoners are entitled to one hour of exercise a day and spend the rest of their time in their cell, with very little access to utilities of any kind.

The Activity Intervention Centre (in G wing, Durham, since May 1999) represents the final stage of the CSC system. It is intended to provide positive activities for prisoners with emphasis on social interaction 'within a well-ordered constructive community ethos'. There is a minimum of 20 hours' constructive activity per week plus a high degree of staff involvement with prisoners. Counselling and cognitive behaviour programmes are also provided for individual prisoners.

Durham I wing provides a regime to manage prisoners who have a history of highly disturbed behaviour, with psychological and psychiatric support. Work, occupational therapy, education, specialist sessions, individual counselling and group work make up the target of 20 hours of constructive activity. On I wing, as at the Activity Intervention and the Programmes Intervention Centres, there is a high degree of staff interaction with prisoners.

Finally, Woodhill D wing serves as the segregation unit for the CSC system, operating a very restricted regime. Prisoners are entitled to one hour's exercise a week, two showers a week and one at the weekend, two 30 minute visits per month, one short pre-booked telephone call midweek and one at the weekend and minimal access to utilities.

Statement of purpose

The original 'Statement of Purpose' in the *Operating Standards for Close Supervision Centres* described their role as follows:

> Close Supervision Centres will operate as part of a national management strategy which aims to secure the return of problematic or disruptive prisoners to a settled and acceptable pattern of institutional behaviour.
>
> 2. The functions of Close Supervision Centres will be

> i)   to remove the most seriously disruptive prisoners from mainstream dispersal or training prisons.

> ii)   to contain highly dangerous or disruptive individuals in small highly supervised units with safety for staff and prisoners.

> iii)   to provide the opportunity for individuals to address their anti-social disruptive behaviour in a controlled environment.

iv)   to stabilise behaviour and prepare for a return to the mainstream with minimum disruption.

Terms of reference

From the outset (as with the former CRC system), the Prison Service decided to commission an independent evaluation of the new CSC system. In the Invitation to Tender for this evaluation, it was specified that the evaluation should include consideration of:

- how the centres are run and managed on a day-to-day basis;

- whether the centres have a beneficial effect on the prisoners; do they increase their chances of being returned to the main system and, if so, does this effect survive their departure from the centres;

- do the centres – as is intended – constitute a genuinely progressive system which is rational and coherent;

- whether the centres are adequately integrated with the rest of the long-term system, both from the management's perspective and from the perspective of individual inmates and their prison careers;

- whether the centres manage to achieve their aims in a humane way;

- whether, as a result of referring people to the centres, order and control within the long-term system is improved (as intended);

- whether those selected for the centres are appropriate for them: there will need to be proper psychiatric assessment of the prisoners in each centre in order to see how far they match their selection criteria – and perhaps to make a rough assessment of whether any inmate is showing signs of deterioration;

- whether the new system is able to accommodate and manage prisoners dealt with under the previous continuous assessment system – in particular what happens to those who cannot be accommodated within the CSC;

- the selection of staff for the centres and the impact which the work has on them – both psychologically and in terms of their careers;

- the 'value added' by the centres to the prison system: the centres will be expensive to set up and maintain and there will need to be a proper assessment of the centres' cost effectiveness in the context of the long-term prison system.

Methods of study

In order to address these wide-ranging terms of reference, the multi-disciplinary research team for the evaluation included mainstream criminologists with extensive experience of prison research (Keith Bottomley, Emma Clare and Alison Liebling), two consultant forensic psychiatrists (Dr Adrian Grounds and Dr Caecilia Taylor) and an economist, as consultant for the cost-effectiveness analysis (Chris Hammond).

The main elements of the research fieldwork and data collection during the two year project were as follows:

(i) *Observation of the day-to-day running of the CSCs:* throughout the duration of the project, Emma Clare made frequent visits to all of the CSCs, when she was able to observe the centres at work, and talk informally to staff and prisoners; these periods of observation totalled 96 days fieldwork, distributed as follows: 15 days in Hull C wing (July – December 1998); 27 days in the Woodhill CSCs (July 1998 – March 1999) and a further 15 days in the second year (November 1999 – March 2000); 15 days in Durham I wing (July – December 1998); 6 days in Durham G wing (May 1999) plus a further 18 days in Durham (November 1999 – March 2000), mainly in G wing, and consulting prisoners' files.

(ii) *Interviews with prisoners and staff:* a systematic programme of interviews with prisoners and staff (including governor grades and specialists) in each centre was carried out by EC (assisted by KB), comprising: 15 prisoners and 31 staff at Woodhill; 5 prisoners and 12 staff at Hull; 10 prisoners and 20 staff at Durham. EC and KB also had discussions and interviews with Prison Service Headquarters staff and the High Security Directorate. In addition (apart from the psychiatric interviews, for which see below) AL interviewed 5 prisoners at Woodhill, including two jointly with one of the psychiatrists (AG), and discussed with senior Prison Service personnel aspects of the history of the management of disruptive prisoners, the Spurr Report etc.

(iii) *Psychiatric interviews:* the consultant forensic psychiatrists (AG and CT) carried out psychiatric assessment interviews (using structured diagnostic schedules) with a total of 23 prisoners, including 14 at Woodhill and nine at Durham; these constituted approximately three-quarters of those resident in the CSCs at the time of the interviews; four prisoners in Woodhill and one in Durham declined to be interviewed.

It should be noted that despite the best efforts by staff it became increasingly difficult to arrange interviews with prisoners at Woodhill in the second year, due to staff shortages and the constraints of the daily routines of the centres; in addition some of the more disruptive prisoners here were moved out to high control cells at short notice, were on dirty protest or deemed by staff to be too dangerous to be interviewed.

(iv) *Documentary material relating to CSC prisoners:* a variety of documentary sources were used to obtain data on the CSC prisoners: referral forms to the CSC Committee; files held on the prisoners in their CSC location; their main records; the incident reporting system; and the local inmate data system.

(v) *Management accounting data* for the cost effectiveness analysis were provided by the finance sections at HMP Durham and HMP Woodhill. Detailed information on the organisation and operation of some Prison Service activities were provided by Headquarters staff, together with details of the related expenditure, where these were not available from published sources or the other fieldwork outlined above.

(vi) *Staff training and in-house evaluation:* Emma Clare attended the two-week team-building and staff training course for CSC staff at Newbold Revel (February 1999); two CSC staff training days (September/October 1999); and two residential in-house CSC evaluation meetings at Harrogate (14–15 October, 1999) and at Peterborough (11–12 April, 2000).

(vii) *CSC Selection Committee and Monitoring Group:* all the monthly meetings of the CSC Selection Committee (February 1998 – April 2000) were attended by EC, as well as the unit managers' meetings; similarly, all the meetings of the CSC Monitoring Group were attended by one or more members of the research team (normally KB or EC).

(viii) *Dispersal prisons and high control cells (HCCs):* visits were made (by KB and/or EC) to each of the five dispersal prisons, in June 1999, to discuss with senior management and specialist staff their views and use of the CSC system during the first 15 months, and the role of HCCs; a series of return visits were made in April/May 2000, to review their experience of the CSC system, including any examples they had of reintegrating CSC prisoners back onto normal location; the opportunity was also taken of interviewing any former CSC prisoners currently being held in the dispersals.

(viii) *Data on order and control in the dispersal estate:* selected data were extracted from from the Order and Control matrix on serious incidents in dispersals for the period before and after the opening of the CSCs.

2. Selection of CSC prisoners and population trends

Prisoner population trends and movements

In its first two years of operation (February 1998 – February 2000) the CSC system managed a total of 51 prisoners. Twelve of these prisoners were already located in special units (formerly CRCs) at Hull and Durham. Seven were being held at Durham and five at Hull at the time of the February 1998 closure of A wing. At least 25 (49%) and possibly as many as 33 (65%) of the 51 prisoners managed by the CSC system had previously been managed by the Continuous Assessment Scheme (CAS).

In the first year, 31 prisoners were referred to the CSC Committee. Fourteen (45%) were accepted by the Committee. Of these, four were selected for I wing Durham CSC and the remaining ten were selected for Woodhill. In the second year of operation (February 1999 – February 2000) 15 prisoners were referred to the CSC Committee. Six of these prisoners were ex-CSC prisoners, including two who had been returned from special hospitals to the prison system. Two of the 15 prisoners were referred to the Committee on more than one occasion. Eight (53%) were accepted by the Committee, with five of the six ex-CSC prisoners being re-selected, although only four of the five eventually ended up back in the system. Six of the prisoners were initially allocated to Woodhill – four to the Structured Regime Centre and two to the Restricted Regime Centre. One prisoner was allocated to Durham I wing and one prisoner was selected for I wing pending an available space.

Woodhill

In its first year of operation, Woodhill opened with four prisoners and gradually built up its numbers. By the end of the first year Woodhill's CSCs and segregation unit (D wing) held 24 prisoners. In its second year, a total of 36 prisoners were managed by Woodhill, with 23 being the lowest and 30 the highest number of prisoners held at any one time. The average population of Woodhill CSCs in the second year was 26 prisoners.

The second year of operation thus saw a stabilisation in the size of the prisoner population at Woodhill. The prisoners there could be broadly divided into four groups: (i) those who generally progressed – 16 (44%); (ii) those who might progress through the CSC system but due to the risk they presented on normal location could not be returned safely to the mainstream – six (17%) ; (iii) those who have progressed through the system but have suffered relatively serious relapses – 6 (17%); and (iv) those who have not co-operated with the system – eight (22%). Whereas in the first year there appeared to be considerable emphasis on moving prisoners through the system quickly, partly due to the lack of activities and programmes available in the centres, this was less evident in the second year.

Although there was little increase in the activities or programmes offered in either the Structured or the Programme Intervention Centre at Woodhill (see below), the extra time spent in one location appeared to have been of benefit, particularly to those prisoners who were cooperating with the system. The emphasis at Woodhill seemed to be moving away from mere behavioural conformity within the system, with more attention given to whether the problems deemed to be the cause of the prisoners' disruptive behaviour still obtained. In terms of the overall aim for the majority of prisoners in the CSC system – returning them to normal location – this change of emphasis seems likely to result in more positive long-term outcomes.

Eleven prisoners spent the second year of the CSCs operation moving between the Restricted Regime (A wing) and the CSC's segregation unit (D wing). Nine of these prisoners spent all of the second year on either the Restricted Regime or the segregation unit, with seven of them also spending periods of time out in dispersal prisons' high control cells. Five of these seven prisoners spent between four and six months each in HCCs between February 1999 and April 2000. Eight of these nine prisoners refused to co-operate with the CSC system for one reason or another, in most cases because they felt they had been inappropriately allocated or considered their presence in the CSC as a form of punishment (rather than an opportunity to address their behaviour). Three of these prisoners spent a considerable period of time moving from A to D and back again over very short periods. The movements of prisoners during the second year are summarised in Table 2.1.

Table 2.1: *Prisoner movements: March 1999 – April 2000*

Management Strategy/Movement of Prisoners	No of Prisoners
Restricted regime	3
Restricted regime + segregation unit	1
Restricted regime + segregation unit + high control cells	5
Segregation unit	1
Segregation unit + high control cells	2
Structured regime + restricted regime + segregation unit	4
Structured regime + programme intervention	2
Structured regime to programme intervention	3
Structured regime to programme intervention to Durham G wing	6
Structured regime to programme intervention to Durham I wing	3
Structured regime to programme intervention to G wing to normal location	2
G wing + structured regime + restricted regime + segregation unit	1
G wing + structured regime + segregation unit + high control cell	1

One prisoner was allocated to D wing, due to the risk he presented to staff and the fact that he appeared to remain relatively stable there, while awaiting a space in a special hospital. Two other prisoners spent considerable periods of the second year on the Restricted Regime and in the segregation unit, with some time in the Structured Regime Centre (three and four months respectively). Both of these prisoners struggled to maintain acceptable behaviour over a sustained period of time.

Three prisoners spent all their time (11 months, 7 months and 7 months, respectively) located in the Restricted Regime Centre. These prisoners were judged to present too high a risk to prisoners and staff in any other conditions, although one was working to address his behavioural problems.

During the second year eight prisoners progressed through the Structured Regime Centre (B wing) and the Programmes Intervention Centre (C wing) at Woodhill and moved on to the Activity Intervention Centre (G wing Durham). Two of these prisoners were subsequently returned to normal location from G wing (October 1999 and April 2000) – one in a local prison and one to normal location in a dispersal. A third prisoner who progressed through Woodhill to Durham G wing was expected to return to normal location fairly soon. A further three prisoners progressed through Woodhill's Structured and Programmes Intervention Centres and moved to I wing, Durham.

Five prisoners spent the second year progressing from the Structured Regime Centre to the Programmes Intervention Centre, with two of these moving back and forth between the two centres. The other three prisoners displayed relatively settled, if still demanding, behaviour. Three prisoners spent their time on the Structured Regime Centre with short periods on A and D wings, and in the case of one prisoner a short period in a high control cell. All three of these prisoners showed more settled behaviour in the early months of 2000, with one of them deemed appropriate for transfer to the Programmes Intervention Centre (C wing). The overall trend during the second year of the CSCs was for prisoners to spend relatively longer periods located both on the Structured Regime Centre and the Programmes Intervention Centre.

Two prisoners were returned from the Activity Intervention Centre (G wing Durham) to Woodhill. One had spent nine months on G wing and the other six months. Although both prisoners were upset about their return they dealt with it differently. Both were disruptive on their return. One later settled down and was attempting to co-operate; it seemed likely that he might soon progress to the Programme Intervention Centre. The other prisoner continued to cause problems, assaulting a member of staff shortly after his return and engaging in a dirty protest, although there were some signs that he might be settling down somewhat. Meanwhile, he remained in the Restricted Regime Centre.

Four prisoners were deselected from the CSC system in its second year whilst located at Woodhill. Two of these prisoners were deselected to special hospitals while a third was deselected to a healthcare centre to await a place in a special hospital. One prisoner was deselected on the grounds of the short time he had left to serve of his sentence.

Durham

G wing opened at Durham in May 1999. In addition to functioning as a CSC it also held a non-CSC high risk prisoner for its first 3–4 months. Due to the fact that G wing came on-stream relatively quickly (following the earlier than expected closure of Hull A wing), and the presence of the high-risk prisoner on the wing, the build-up of prisoners was relatively slow. Beginning with two ex-Hull CSC prisoners the population built up to seven over its first year of operation (by April 2000). Two prisoners progressed through Woodhill and G wing and were deselected from G wing to normal location (October 1999 and April 2000). Two prisoners were returned from G wing to Woodhill following sustained periods of disruptive behaviour which was destabilising the Centre.

Three of the prisoners located on G wing were deemed to be long-term prisoners who, due to the risk they would present there, were unlikely to progress to normal location for the foreseeable future. Their behaviour within the CSC system was, however, considered appropriate and they had complied with its requirements. Of the remaining three, one was expected to transfer to Whitemoor in the near future and the other two prisoners were in the process of having more detailed re-integration plans drawn up for them to work towards. As this was G wing's first year of operation, much of the time was spent establishing protocols and systems and acclimatising staff to their new role within a CSC

For most of its first year I wing had operated at one below its maximum capacity of nine prisoners. In its second year I wing managed an average of eight prisoners, with its lowest number being six. One prisoner was deselected to a special hospital in May 1999. Four prisoners spent all the period, February 1999 –April 2000, located on I wing. Three prisoners progressed from Woodhill to I wing during the second year and one prisoner was selected for I wing directly from Wakefield segregation unit.

One prisoner was due to be released from I wing in May 2000. It had been operating at full capacity since October 1999 and at the time of writing there were two prisoners awaiting spaces there, one located at Woodhill (C wing) and one in Wakefield segregation unit.

Prisoner selection

Entry to the CSC system is restricted
    to those prisoners who have a history of disruptive and aggressive behaviour and who
    meet one or more of the following criteria (i.e. prisoners who have):
    been violent to prisoners and staff
    regularly incurred disciplinary reports
    caused serious damage to property in prison
    shown dangerous behaviour (such as roof top protests or hostage taking)
    failed to respond to earlier measures to improve control
    been on continuous segregation under Rule 43 (GOAD) for a period of three months or more.
                    (Close Supervision Operating Standards, Annexe 1, 21.4.1999).

Of the 51 prisoners managed within the system to date, it was possible to obtain some degree of information on the criminal histories and previous prison behaviour of 41 of them. Nine of the prisoners were no longer being managed by the CSC system when the data collection occurred and therefore information was no longer easily accessible for these prisoners. Only very limited information could be found on another prisoner; but where it is available it is included and therefore 42 prisoners may be referred to on occasion.

A variety of sources were used to obtain data on the CSC prisoners: referral forms to the CSC Committee; files held on the prisoners in their CSC location; their main records; the incident reporting system; and the local inmate data system. The data recorded in any one of these sites were in no way comprehensive, as there were often large gaps in the prisoners' histories, and in many cases the information recorded was not always sufficient enough to allow for a detailed analysis of the prisoner's history. Thus, the following statements relate to the 41 (or 42) prisoners for whom varying amounts of information were available.

Prisoner characteristics

All but two of the 41 prisoners had originally been convicted of violent offences. Twenty two of the prisoners had been convicted of murder, another two had been convicted of manslaughter, and four were serving sentences for attempted murder. Four prisoners were serving sentences for armed robbery and four for robbery. Two prisoners were convicted of wounding with intent and one of aggravated burglary. Two of the prisoners were serving sentences for conspiracy to rob (see Table 2.2).

Table 2.2: Main offences of CSC prisoners

Main Offence	Prisoners
Murder	22
Manslaughter	2
Attempted murder	4
Armed robbery	4
Robbery	4
Wounding with intent	2
Aggravated burglary	1
Conspiracy to rob	2

Twenty-five of the prisoners were serving life sentences, two of which were 'natural life' sentences. Ten of these prisoners had tariff recommendations recorded: six had been recommended to serve 20 years; two 15 years; one 12 years and one eight years. Of the prisoners serving determinate sentences, 12 were serving between 10 to 20 years and two prisoners were serving over 20 but less than 30 years (see Table 2.3).

Table 2.3: Length of sentence of CSC prisoners

Sentence Length	Prisoners
Life ('natural life')	2
Life (recorded tariffs of 8–20 years)	23
20 – 30 years	2
10 –20 years	12

Twenty-seven of the prisoners were sentenced between 1990 and 1996, nine between 1984 and 1989 and four between 1975 and 1983 (see Table 2.4).

Table 2.4: Year of Sentence of CSC prisoners

Year Sentenced	Prisoners Sentenced
1996	4
1995	5
1994	0
1993	10
1992	5
1991	1
1990	3
1989	2
1988	1
1987	1
1986	1
1985	2
1984	2
1983	1
1982	0
1981	1
1980	1
1979	0
1978	0
1977	0
1976	0
1975	1

Application of selection criteria

Six of the prisoners had killed whilst in prison, including one on more than one occasion. A seventh prisoner had been charged with the murder of a fellow prisoner. In addition, five of the prisoners had committed acts of serious violence against prisoners or staff. Four prisoners had taken hostages and one prisoner had been involved in a roof top climb. Twenty-seven of the prisoners had adjudications for assaults against staff, prisoners or both. Another 13 prisoners had adjudications that would identify them as being 'subversive' and 'threatening'.

Although the vast majority of prisoners did in practice match the selection criteria for the CSC system, it might nevertheless be argued that the process of selection had not always been entirely appropriate, particularly in the first year of the system's operation. Almost half (49%) of the prisoners originally selected for the CSC system were taken from the Continuous Assessment Scheme (CAS). These prisoners had experienced months, and in many cases years, of moving from segregation unit to segregation unit under this scheme. It proved extremely difficult to establish how long prisoners had been on CAS from the information available or exactly why they were originally placed on it.

However, the fact that a prisoner was on CAS appeared in many cases to have been the sole de facto reason for the prisoner's selection for the CSC system. Unless it was for very obvious reasons (i.e. causing a death or a very serious assault or form of disorder) it was quite often the case that the original reasons for the prisoner being placed on CAS were lost by the time the prisoner's case came before the CSC Selection Committee. This has had repercussions in terms of defending legal challenges by prisoners regarding their allocation to the CSC system, and in terms of some prisoners' perception of the fairness and justice of the system and their allocation. Many of the prisoners could not recall the reasons for their original placement on CAS or considered them to be so far in the past that being placed now in the CSC system was perceived as an additional punishment for something they had already been punished for.

Information for selection

In terms of analysing whether the prisoners matched the official selection criteria, disciplinary records should have been one of the main sources of information. Whilst this allowed us to ascertain the numbers and types of disciplinary offences the prisoners had committed, very little circumstantial information was recorded regarding the incidents. For example, it would simply be recorded that the prisoner assaulted staff, damaged property or used threatening or abusive words, language or behaviour. Rarely was there any indication of the seriousness of the assault, the level of damage or the nature of the threats or abuse; nor was there any contextual information regarding the disciplinary offences of the prisoners or their disruptive behaviour more generally.

This was also the case with the periods the prisoners had spent in segregation units on R43 Good Order and Against Discipline (GOAD). Although many of the CSC prisoners had spent considerable periods segregated it was often very hard to establish the original events leading up to the need to segregate them and the reasons for continuing their segregation. They were seen as disruptive prisoners, and while this was indeed the case, the specific environments and contexts in which they have been disruptive are of importance. The recording of the contexts in which disruptive behaviour occurs could well offer ideas as to how to successfully manage the prisoners whilst in the CSC system and help them avoid difficulties in the future. It might also allow situations which are common flashpoints for disruptive behaviour amongst prisoners to be identified and solutions for the better management of such situations to be devised.

At a CSC staff away-day, 'Starting from a position of knowledge' was identified as where the CSC system ought to have been operating from. Despite the fact that all of the prisoners in the system had been in the prison system a minimum of four years (see Table 2.4 above) very little accumulated knowledge existed regarding the prisoners and their behaviour. The majority of the prisoners may have been well known to staff and managers and their reputations as disruptive prisoners well known throughout the system but a detailed record of how and why the prisoners had ended up in the CSC system was largely absent. While recognising the large numbers the Prison Service manages on a daily basis and acknowledging the fact that this leads to a recording system not geared toward developing detailed information on prisoners, at least until 1992 and the advent of Sentence Plans, this absence of accumulated knowledge on the CSC prisoners is detrimental both to the selection procedure (it makes decisions harder to defend when challenged legally) and the management of prisoners within the system (many of the prisoners are an unknown quantity when they arrive).

The minutes of the CSC Selection Committee were not as useful as they could have been for the evaluation and monitoring of the selection process. Although the minutes provided a descriptive record of the prisoners' behaviour within the system, little detail was recorded in terms of the management strategies attempted with the prisoners and the success or not of these strategies. More comprehensive minutes of Committee meetings would enable best practices to be identified and exchanged between the different centres. Furthermore, the fuller recording of decisions and management strategies within the CSC system would also be of benefit when the CSC system is legally challenged by prisoners.

Whilst the initial selection criteria for the CSC system were clearly identified and adhered to, the criteria on which decisions were made to progress prisoners through the system were less apparent. Decisions to progress, and in some cases downgrade, prisoners could seem arbitrary and dependent on whether the Committee was 'favourable' towards a particular prisoner. This sense of arbitrariness could be removed if more objective and clearly identified criteria for progressing prisoners were identified. Once an understanding of the prisoners' behaviour has been developed within the system it would be possible to assess individual prisoners against the objective criteria and ascertain whether, for this prisoner, the criteria of progression have been met.

Selection process

The process of selection to the CSC system improved during the second year of operation. If there was uncertainty about the quality of the referral forms or if key sections (for example psychiatric reports) were missing, then decisions to select were invariably deferred until that information was available. The information contained within referral forms and the quality of that information provided are important since it is from this that the decision to allocate a prisoner and the beginnings of management strategies are made.

Recent referrals from Wakefield segregation unit were examples of good practice in this respect. They contained the basic information regarding reasons for referral, disciplinary records, periods of segregation, wing and psychology reports and so on, and they also contained good quality information about the prisoners themselves and their attitudes/state of mind at the time of selection. In these cases, Wakefield staff had been working with the prisoners for a period of time and had developed a good understanding of the prisoners, enabling them in some cases to begin preparatory work with the prisoners, prior to their transfer into the CSC system.

For prisoners who are about to enter the CSC system this preparatory work seems important; prisoners who understand why and where they are being transferred and how it might benefit them may be more amenable to co-operating with the system. At the very least it would avoid the confusion prisoners experienced in the early days of the CSC system when they did not appear to understand what the system was for or why they were there.

Inclusion of prison officers from the centres at CSC Selection Committee meetings was another example of good practice. Attendance at these meetings offered a view of the overall workings of the system and highlighted the sensitive nature of the decisions being made by the Committee. It offered a regular forum for centre staff and Prison Service Headquarters personnel to exchange views and concerns in a constructive manner and this process of open communication is one that should be maintained and encouraged.

Prisoners not accommodated within the CSCs

Our terms of reference invited us to address the issue of whether the new CSC system has been able to accommodate and manage prisoners dealt with under the previous Continuous Assessment Scheme (CAS), and in particular what happens to those who cannot be accommodated within the CSCs. We discuss elsewhere in this Report how successful the CSC system has been in dealing with those former CAS prisoners who were selected for transfer into the CSCs. In this section we summarise our findings about three other groups of prisoners: (i) former CAS prisoners who were not selected for the CSC system, (ii) prisoners referred to the CSC Selection Committee (February 1998 – April 2000) but not selected, and (iii) those prisoners who have been deselected from the CSC system, to date.

Unselected CAS prisoners
Seventeen (45%) of the 38 prisoners who were listed as being on the Continuous Assessment Scheme in February 1998, when the CSC system was established, were not in fact transferred to the CSCs, but dealt with in some alternative way.

One was released from prison directly from CAS, having completed his sentence, and another prisoner was transferred to a special hospital. The other 15 former CAS prisoners were transferred to normal location during 1998, and were not later referred to or selected for CSCs. Apart from one prisoner, who assaulted a prison officer in Frankland but was subsequently transferred to Full Sutton where he was not involved in any further acts of violence, none of the other prisoners for whom we were able to check their disciplinary records had any proven charges of violence or seriously disruptive behaviour.

Thus, we were able to conclude that virtually all those prisoners who were in CAS at the beginning of 1998 but not subsequently selected for the CSC system (before CAS formally closed in February 1999) appeared to have settled down on normal location, either within the dispersal system or (in a few cases) outwith the dispersals.

CSC referrals who were not accepted

Twenty three (50%) of the 46 prisoners who were new referrals to the CSC Selection Committee in its first two years were initially rejected by the Committee as not suitable for transfer to the CSCs. Three of these prisoners were subsequently re-referred and accepted into the CSC system. We were able to follow-up the majority of the remaining 20 prisoners, and discovered something about their subsequent prison behaviour.

Sixteen (75%) of the rejected prisoners were held within the dispersal system on normal location, without causing any serious trouble – as far as their official disciplinary records accurately reflected sthis. Four prisoners were on normal location outside the dispersal estate. In only four of the 20 cases was there any evidence of any serious recurring trouble, that might have (but did not in practice) merit re-referral to the CSC Selection Committee. In six cases, the prisoners had two or fewer proven disciplinary charges, of a non-violent nature.

It can be concluded, therefore, that the CSC selection process was generally very successful in identifying those prisoners referred to the Committee who did not pose a serious risk to other prisoners or staff and therefore did not need to be managed within the CSC system.

Prisoners deselected from CSCs

The final group of prisoners that come within the remit of this discussion, but some of whom are also considered elsewhere in this Report, are those prisoners who were deselected from the CSCs during the period under review. A total of 15 prisoners were recorded as being deselected from the CSCs, between February 1998 and March 2000.

Four of these prisoners were deselected in order to be transferred to a special hospital. However, two of these prisoners were involved in violent incidents which led to their being referred back to the CSCs, where they seemed fairly settled. It is difficult deciding whether transfers to special hospitals should be generally regarded as 'successes' or 'failures' of the CSC system. On balance, they should probably be considered 'successes', as it is clear that there will always be a relatively small but significant group of disruptive prisoners who can and should be better managed and treated in special hospitals than by the Prison Service.

Five (45%) of the remaining 11 deselected prisoners subsequently failed on normal location, were re-referred and transferred back into the CSC system. We were able to obtain up-to-date information on four of the other six prisoners, appearing to confirm that they were reasonably settled and stable on normal location in a variety of prisons, viz. Bullingdon, Doncaster, Durham and Full Sutton.

Conclusion

It does seem, therefore, that the CSC Selection Committee has been fairly good at identifying the worst risks both among the former CAS prisoners and from those who have been referred to it since February 1998, so that few of the CAS prisoners or rejected referrals have caused further serious trouble. On the other hand, the 'success rate' of those prisoners who have been through the CSC system and been deselected has not been impressive – with only a handful of the prisoners released back into the mainstream (or to special hospitals) being able to survive for long without getting involved in further violence or seriously disruptive behaviour.

3. Regimes and management of the centres

Two of the Operating Principles for Close Supervision Centres (as set out in the Operating Standards) relate to the nature and purpose of regimes in CSCs:

4. CSC staff will actively engage with prisoners to encourage and assist them to address their disruptive behaviour. Team working and individual prisoner case management will be the key features of these arrangements.

5. CSCs will provide a co-ordinated range of regimes to manage seriously disruptive prisoners. The regimes aim to facilitate change and encourage improved behaviour. CSC regimes will operate within a framework of incentives and earned privileges. Enhanced level privileges will not be available within the CSC system.

When the Close Supervision Centre system was first opened in February 1998 it was intended that the centres and their regimes would provide a progressive path for prisoners to work their way through, with the ultimate aim of returning to normal location in mainstream prisons. Although removing disruptive prisoners from dispersal or training prisons and containing them in conditions where safety of staff and prisoners could be maintained was also a primary objective, the original conception and the emphasis in the early days of the CSCs was very much on progressing prisoners up through the different levels of the system and returning them to the mainstream. The centres, with their differing regimes, would offer prisoners both the opportunity to address their disruptive behaviour and incentives to encourage them to address their problems and return to normal location.

Four of the five centres were seen to make up the core of this progressive system: the Structured Regime Centre (B wing), the Programmes Intervention Centre (C wing), and the Restricted Regime Centre (A wing) at Woodhill, plus the Activity Intervention Centre (original located at Hull, A wing, now located at Durham, G wing). I wing at Durham had the more specialised role of managing prisoners with a history of highly disturbed behaviour and as such had a more self-contained role within the CSC system. All prisoners would initially be allocated to the Structured Regime Centre at Woodhill and then, dependent on their behaviour, progress through the system.

Woodhill

Although many avenues were explored to address them, many of the problems and difficulties identified during Woodhill's first year of operation persisted throughout its second year. Regime delivery continued to be a problem in the second year, as Woodhill was unable to meet the standards of provision specified for the different Centres.

C wing – Programmes Intervention Centre

Throughout most of the second year the Programmes Intervention Centre (C wing) failed to offer any constructive activity for a sustained period; prisoners generally spent their hours out of cell playing board games or watching television. As in the first year, attempts were made to increase the level of constructive activity; part of the second floor was converted into an education/computer room and towards the end of the fieldwork (March 2000) the finishing touches were being put to a room which had been converted into a crafts room. Once this is functional, prisoners will either take part in the crafts activity or remain in their cells.

In addition to these changes, staff from Woodhill visited both I and G wing at Durham in an attempt to develop the regime on offer in the Programmes Intervention Centre (and to ensure compatibility between C and G wings). Although various ideas and suggestions were made following these visits, for introducing some of the activities and practices already in use on I or G wing, there was a considerable delay before these were put in place in Woodhill. It was only towards the end of the second year of operation that significant activities began to be introduced in the Programmes Intervention Centre.

Efforts to enhance the regime were additionally hampered by the continual shut downs of the centres, often at short notice, due to staffing shortages (see below). As in the first year, C wing was often closed in afternoons and/or evenings, which interfered with the process of developing a constructive environment for prisoners and staff. This continued lack of constructive activity meant there was minimal interaction between prisoners and staff and when it did occur it mainly consisted of routine activities such as supervising exercise or mealtimes.

Provision of group work

In addition to the general lack of constructive activity, there was very little provision of group work on C wing during the first two years of operation. Two Enhanced Thinking Skills (ETS) courses took place, one at the end of January 1999 and one during July/August 1999. As noted in our Interim Report (July, 1999), a major preoccupation for the first part of the first year of operation for Psychology was whether or not group work could be provided for prisoners in CSCs, as a considerable number of the prisoners were obtaining high scores on the Psychopathy Checklist. Opinion differed on whether or not group work can be detrimental to those who have high psychopathy scores. After much debate a compromise position was adopted whereby group work could be conducted with prisoners in the CSC but it would not be accredited group work.

Since its implementation, the ETS course designed for CSC prisoners has been evaluated and it is expected that it will receive accreditation in the near future. However, the logistical problems of actually providing ETS courses to CSC prisoners remain. It was difficult to identify groups of prisoners who fitted the criteria and yet were both large enough and compatible enough for satisfactory delivery of the course – hence it had only been possible to run two courses in the first two years.

Efforts were made to address this difficulty by exploring the possibility of offering the ETS course to a combination of B and C wing prisoners (despite the issue of prisoner compatibility) and there were plans to introduce such a course in the near future. In addition there were plans to introduce more basic preparatory courses onto B wing, such as those exploring basic social and communication skills and preparing prisoners for the experience of carrying out group work. None of these courses had yet been introduced. Considering the nature of the social, emotional and in many cases mental health difficulties of this group of prisoners, an emphasis on courses that attempt to address these basic concerns would probably be a more profitable investment of psychological resources.

Moreover, a number of prisoners interviewed who had completed the ETS questioned its relevance and usefulness; a number pointed out that they had only taken part in it so that they could ensure their transfer to Durham. Others, however, did find it useful. There could be more staff involvement in such courses, which might both enhance staff roles on B and C wing and increase the level of interaction between prisoners and staff. Although the emphasis of psychological courses and group work in prisons is to provide accredited work, perhaps there should be a more flexible approach to psychological work with CSC prisoners, in view of the extreme nature of their difficulties.

Lack of constructive activities

Both staff and prisoners continued to suffer from high levels of boredom on C wing. Prisoners appeared to express less frustration about the level of activities and group work than in the first year; there appeared to be lower expectations from prisoners regarding receiving help in addressing their disruptive behaviour. Staff, however, continued to experience and express high levels of frustration about not being able to carry out the work they felt they should be doing, working with prisoners through activities and group work to help them address their behaviour.

The lack of activities and staff-prisoner interaction on C wing created difficulties for prisoners who eventually moved to Durham G wing. A number of the prisoners interviewed in G wing identified a large gap between the regimes of the two wings. Consequently, a number of them struggled to make the transition from C wing with its low level of activity and interaction to G wing, where prisoners were expected to be constructively occupied all day and where staff presence, and often involvement, in activities was the norm. It was a culture shock to the prisoners, some of whom noted that they needed several weeks to acclimatise to the change, and as a result their behaviour could at first deteriorate due to the pressure of the change.

B wing – Structured Regime Centre

The role of the Structured Regime Centre (B wing) within the CSC system was to provide an assessment of prisoners on their arrival to the system and to offer prisoners some opportunity to participate in constructive activities and personal development. In an attempt to improve the assessment process a more thorough and comprehensive assessment tool was piloted on B wing in August 1999. This was a modified version of the Dispersal Induction Assessment (DIA) scheme recently introduced in all dispersal prisons, which included assessment of educational, psychological and throughcare needs. Although there had been little evidence of the new assessment scheme having much impact upon B wing, its potential usefulness should not be underestimated.

Given the limited information available on the majority of prisoners (see above), it is important that more knowledge about the prisoners is obtained prior to their arrival in the CSC system. If used effectively this improved assessment could highlight areas of concern that the prisoner has about his situation (thereby encouraging a degree of personal investment on the part of the prisoners) and it would provide those whose responsibility it is to manage the prisoner with a better understanding of the prisoner. It is important, however, that the purpose and benefits of completing such an assessment are made clear to the prisoner so that it does not become interpreted by prisoners as another method for managing and controlling them. It is also vital that the information that is collected on prisoners is transferred with them on progression in order to ensure a continuity of work with the prisoners.

In addition, the information gathered from the initial assessments could be used to inform the types of programmes and courses that are planned to be introduced onto B wing in the future (see above). To date virtually no constructive activity and personal development activities have taken place on B wing (except for personal officer interviews and one-to-one psychology interviews). If programmes and courses are to be introduced it is better that they are based on reliable information about the prisoners rather than on partial knowledge and assumptions about their backgrounds and needs.

As with all the centres at Woodhill in the second year, the Structured Regime Centre continued to struggle simply to deliver the basic day-to-day regime. The process of unlocking prisoners one at a time for meals, unlocking prisoners for cleaning, the routine for showering and exercising prisoners meant that staff often found it very difficult to complete their basic handling tasks. There was little time, or opportunity, to engage with prisoners beyond the fulfilment of routine activities. As on C wing, when prisoners were out of their cells on association the majority of them would spend most of their time in the television room, and hence very little meaningful staff-prisoner interaction occurred; although some prisoners would actively seek out staff to talk to during their association periods. Staff felt that the regime on B wing at best allowed them to elicit a more settled pattern of behaviour from prisoners but it gave them no opportunity to assess in any systematic way their behaviour and/or the problems that gave rise to their disruptive behaviour.

A wing – Restricted Regime Centre

When the CSC system first opened, the Restricted Regime Centre (A wing) was undoubtedly seen as being part of the progressive element of Woodhill CSCs. Although prisoners were being kept in extremely restricted conditions, staff were still expected to encourage them to address their disruptive behaviour and encourage them to move back up to B wing.

The regime on A wing elicited extremely negative and confrontational reactions from the prisoners from the outset. The conditions on A wing when it first opened were initially lower that those to be found in a dispersal segregation unit and prisoners considered it unjust for them to be placed in these conditions. Furthermore, many of them considered that the incentives on offer to them to progress were insulting or degrading. These factors, combined with prisoners feeling they should not have been allocated to the CSC system in the first place, led to a number of prisoners adopting a strong 'non-compliance' stance.

Although the conditions on A wing were changed, in the revised Operating Standards (April 1999), to equate with conditions found in dispersal segregation units, the prisoners' original perception of the system as unjust and punitive remained largely unaltered and they persisted in their increasingly aggressive protest against the system throughout the second year of operation.

D wing – the effects of the protests

The continual non-conforming, challenging and often assaultive behaviour of this relatively small number of prisoners had a number of serious repercussions on the operation of all the Woodhill centres and the overall management of the CSC system during its first two years. These non-compliant prisoners occupied much of the time and energy of staff and management at all levels of the CSC system, often to the detriment of the regime needs and resources of B and C wing. Their behaviour led to the emergence of D wing – initially designated as the segregation unit for the whole system – as a long-term containment unit for those prisoners protesting against the system most vociferously.

As a result, this unintentional role for D wing somewhat limited the options for dealing with more 'ordinary' displays of disruptive behaviour in the CSCs. Management was reluctant to use the segregation unit as it would be used in a normal long-term prison and there were frequently very few spaces available on D wing. In any case, placing prisoners there for punishment purposes risked them being negatively influenced by the persistent non-conformers already located on D wing.

Control vs progression?

The concerted indiscipline and extensive dirty protests of this group of prisoners on A and D wings led directly to a polarisation of the notions of 'control' versus 'progression'. As it became apparent during the first year that a relatively large number of prisoners (in relation to the number in the system at that time) were unwilling to co-operate or prepared to progress through the system, an additional (fifth) function was added to the role of the CSC system in the revised Operating Standards: viz. "to contain for as long as necessary any prisoner presenting so great a threat to the safety of staff and prisoners that long-term containment is the only option available" (Statement of Purpose, 2.v).

The introduction of this new function for the CSCs was interpreted as endorsing the control/containment role of A and D wings at Woodhill, in contrast to the 'progression' function of B and C wings. Thus, by the beginning of its second year of operation Woodhill CSCs had split into two distinct halves, operating on opposing principles.

The containment of high-risk prisoners

This additional function also highlighted the increasingly acknowledged need for providing an appropriate location and regime for the small number of prisoners who may well progress quite quickly through the CSC system but were clearly not suitable for return to normal location in the mainstream. As a consequence, within what was still essentially intended as a progressive system, A wing has had to manage prisoners who, although they may conform to the regime, could not be progressed in the normal way because of the risk they presented. At the same time A wing (with D wing) had to contain those prisoners who were refusing to co-operate and continually challenged the system.

The presence of the 'non-compliant' prisoners destabilised the operation of A wing and unsettled those prisoners on A wing who were either conforming or attempting to address their difficult behaviour and move on through the system. In a short space of time, therefore, and with no additional preparation or training for staff, the characteristics and role of A wing had changed considerably.

Similarly, although D wing was never envisaged as a centre, for much of the first two years it functioned as a long-term containment Centre for the most aggressive, demanding and non-conforming of the CSC prisoners. Given that there were no plans to use D wing in this manner, staff and management struggled to develop a role for D wing beyond the containment of prisoners, in increasingly oppressive conditions for prisoners and staff. In practice, there were no clear objectives beyond containment for D wing and as the prisoners' protests, aggressive and intimidating behaviour and occasionally assaultive behaviour in no way diminished during the second year (and in many cases increased), staff and management concerns over what to do with these prisoners escalated.

Perhaps most importantly, through a combination of prisoners' behaviour and staff and management responses to their behaviour, staff engagement and interaction with prisoners on D wing, and with those non-conforming prisoners located on A wing, had completely broken down. While in many ways it was understandable both how and why this happened, it became increasingly harder for staff to engage with prisoners who showed such contempt for them and who continually threatened and intimidated them. Without some avenue of communication being opened with these prisoners it is difficult to envisage how to move beyond the hostile stalemate that has been reached.

Durham

G wing – Activity Intervention Centre

The Activity Intervention Centre was relocated to G wing Durham in May 1999. Although Durham G wing was being considered as a temporary (and possible long-term) location for the centre whilst Hull was being refurbished, the unexpected early closure of the Hull unit meant that G wing became the permanent location much earlier than anticipated. As a result, there was little time (under two months) for preparation for the considerable changes that needed to be made to G wing, both physically and in terms of staff roles and expectations, to convert it into a CSC.

G wing originally operated as a high-risk Cat A segregation unit and considerable reconstruction work was required to make the area more suitable for its new role as a CSC. In addition there was inadequate provision in terms of staff facilities. There were also plans to convert a self-contained part of the wing into special accommodation for a high-risk non-CSC prisoner who was still located on G wing. Consequently G wing opened up whilst considerable construction work was going on and although the prisoner population was relatively low at the time these were not ideal conditions under which to open the centre.

In addition to the physical alterations, there was little time to prepare the staff for their new role. Staff were expected to go from operating a regime where prisoners were locked up for the majority of the time to a regime where prisoners were unlocked for the majority of the time and high levels of staff-prisoner interaction were expected. The presence of the high-risk non-CSC prisoner on the wing further complicated the opening and operation of the centre, as completely separate unlocking, exercise, and education periods were required for this prisoner. A number of the prisoners also expressed some concern about the prisoner being located on the wing and the fact that although this prisoner had a history of disruptive behaviour unlike them he had not had to work his way up through the CSC system.

Given these circumstances it is unsurprising that initially there was a degree of uncertainty amongst staff about their role and, for some, concern about their safety. Some of the prisoners attempted to undermine staff by constantly pointing out that Durham was not running as Hull used to. It is to the credit of CSC managers at Durham and the G wing staff that this period of uncertainty and instability was relatively short-lived.

All the staff were interviewed by management regarding their suitability for and interest in continuing to work on G wing following its role change. Over a period of time those staff who did not feel committed to working in a CSC were moved off and replaced. As many of the G wing staff as possible were sent on the national CSC training course as soon as possible so that they would be clearer about and more confident in their new role. The CSC manager maintained daily contact with the centre offering support and advice to staff., whilst prisoner numbers were built up slowly. G wing also had the benefit of drawing from the staff and regime of I wing, which had already been proved to work successfully.

Regime delivery

Education, cookery, crafts and the gym were the core features of the Activity Intervention Centre's regime. Five two and a half hour sessions of education and two cookery sessions (two and a half hours) were provided per week and the gym equipment was available for use most days. There were two computers based on G wing and these were the primary focus of education classes, although one prisoner was preparing for exams in maths. Space continued to be a problem in terms of regime provision, for example some of the prisoners ended up using the table tennis table for their crafts or book work.

The location of the gym equipment hindered delivery of the regime to some extent. Due to its open location on the ground floor (almost directly in front of the education rooms) the sound level of the prisoners working out, accompanied by music, could often overpower the whole wing. Its presence also cluttered up the lower ground floor and limited the space available for interaction there. Bids have been put in for a separate gym room to be constructed adjacent to the yard to alleviate this problem, and relocation of the gym equipment would improve the overall working of the wing considerably, providing more working and social space on the ground floor.

As with I wing, it was policy for staff to sit-in on all the classes and in some cases take an active part in them. Since many of the staff had interests in computers and the gym these were the areas where most staff involvement occurred. Through staff involvement with the gym in particular, there developed a considerable degree of staff-prisoner interaction. Despite the somewhat macho and competitive element of the prisoner-staff work-outs, there were undoubtedly a number of cases where this initially low level of interaction led to the development of positive staff-prisoner relations.

Group work and the role of psychology

One area in which the Activity Intervention Centre was unable to meet its stipulated regime provision was in providing counselling and cognitive behaviour programmes to individual prisoners. Only limited psychological input, both in terms of providing counselling or programmes for prisoners and advice and support to management and staff in their dealings with prisoners, had been available since G wing opened. For almost a year Durham prison was without a psychology department. Despite numerous advertisements and other avenues being explored it was only in April 2000 that psychologists were finally recruited to the prison.

Towards the end of 1999 a psychologist was recruited on a consultancy basis to provide some psychological input to I wing. This psychologist also began some basic work with two prisoners on G wing in the early months of 2000. This failure to provide the psychological input as stipulated in the Operating Standards (Principle 5: Regimes) was a considerable handicap. Not only did it prevent those prisoners who were genuinely interested in addressing their behaviour from doing so, it provided those prisoners who were less motivated with ammunition with which to criticise the centre. It is particularly important that management and staff should be offered some input from specialists with an understanding of these prisoners' behaviour in order to assist them in programme and regime delivery, and to increase their awareness of the ways in which prisoners can manipulate and undermine staff confidence.

Re-entry to the mainstream

G wing staff spent much of the first year establishing the regime and systems, and in becoming acclimatised to their new role. They gradually reached the stage where more thought was being given to the process of reintegrating prisoners back onto normal location and what the key requirements of this process might be. With the return of two prisoners to normal location during the first year staff and management had some 'test cases' which they could build on and learn from. The importance of the transition of prisoner to normal location in a different prison had already been identified and ways of improving that process were being explored. Although one act of concerted indiscipline amongst prisoners took place on G wing in its first year of operation, which lead to a Tornado team being on standby outside the wing, staff were able to resolve the incident without their involvement. Despite a number of concerns continuing to exist amongst staff (see Staffing Issues) a level of stability appeared to have been reached relatively quickly on G wing.

I wing

I wing has always had the more specialised role of managing those CSC prisoners with a history of highly disturbed behaviour (with the roots being considered to be mental health problems) and as such had a more self-contained role within the CSC system. I wing was intended to provide a therapeutic regime with psychological and psychiatric support. Work, occupational therapy, education, specialist sessions, individual counselling and group work made up the target 20 hours of constructive activity. To accommodate the different psychological needs of the prisoners on I wing a much more individualised approach had to be adopted within the parameters of the general regime structure.

Computers, the gym and crafts have remained the cornerstones of I wing's regime. The high level of staff interaction with prisoners, established in the first year, was maintained throughout the second year. A relaxed and dynamic environment continued to flourish on the wing, with unobtrusive but firm control established and maintained through the interpersonal skills of the staff. Staff interest and commitment to helping prisoners was recognised by many of the prisoners and this in turn encouraged them to cooperate and become involved in the regime.

Psychological and psychiatric support

There was, however, a significant weakening in the regime provision through the lack of any full-time specialist psychological support. From June 1999 I wing was without any full-time psychological input, although interim provision was established late in 1999 in the form of a clinical psychologist from a local secure unit attending weekly staff meetings. Although this was useful, it did not compensate for the absence of individual and group work with prisoners which had been an integral part of the regime in the first year.

Many attempts were made to recruit suitable psychologists to the prison but it was not until March 2000 that a suitable person was appointed. At the time of writing a psychologist had yet to be allocated to work in the CSCs. The problem of recruiting experienced psychologists is in no way limited to the CSC system but is a Service-wide problem. Although a number of prisoners felt the absence of a psychologist, and the opportunity to work through some of their problems, it was a credit to the psychiatric nurse and uniformed staff that they continued to maintain the stable behaviour of the prisoners located on I wing in the absence of specialist psychological support.

Variations and comparisons between the centres

As in the first year, the quality of regimes and the ability of the different centres to provide regimes varied throughout the second year of the CSC system. I wing continued to build upon the stabilising environment it established in the first year. G wing, although experiencing teething problems, appeared to be developing a similar stable and interactive environment along the lines of I wing. The Woodhill centres, however, despite continued investment by staff and the exploration of solutions by management, struggled to provide even the basics of each of their centre regimes. In terms of developing as an integrated system there were clear indications that the Woodhill centres and the centres at Durham were beginning to evolve along rather separate lines, and were occasionally at odds with each other.

Building upon a first year in which a constructive regime and good working relationships with prisoners were established in I wing, the staff of both I and G wings at Durham developed a secure confidence within their centres that enabled them to explore ways in which they could further develop and enhance their positive work with prisoners. The Woodhill centres, on the other hand, had yet to reach this level of stability. Staff continued to be preoccupied by the day-to-day running of the centres and there had not yet emerged a settled period within the centres that would allow staff to consolidate their experiences and move beyond focusing simply on the delivery of daily routines.

Physical separation and operational autonomy
There appeared to be a number of factors linked to the differences in the centres' evolution. Although I and G wing are located in the same prison they are physically separate and, more importantly perhaps, staffed independently of each other. Both centres had always been adequately staffed. Both I and G wing had clearly identified roles; I wing to provide a therapeutic environment for disruptive prisoners who have mental health problems at the root of their disruptiveness and G wing to prepare prisoners for reintegration into mainstream prison.

Both centres at Durham delivered structured regimes, with considerable staff-prisoner interaction. From the outset both centres had strong management, and despite managerial changes the style of management remained the same to date (a second change in managers took place in April 2000). Staff felt that their managers had clear and realistic expectations about what could be achieved. They felt listened to and supported by their immediate managers and felt they were treated with respect. Whenever possible, staff were consulted before decisions were made and the reasons for the decisions made were fed back to staff. Strong management support and a willingness to allow Durham staff openly to discuss problems and difficulties led to a high degree of confidence amongst staff on I wing and increasing confidence on G wing, resulting in a good team spirit in both centres.

In contrast, although there were three separate centres located at Woodhill, the CSCs there had never really had the opportunity to function as individual Centres. This had a number of repercussions in terms of managing the prisoners within the centres, the staff who work in the centres and the regimes provided.

The CSCs at Woodhill were located physically within one building (Houseblock 6) and had always been managed as one unit rather than as the three separate centres, plus a segregation unit, that they were. In addition the staff for the centres were provided from one pool and, although it was always intended to allocate staff to individual centres, due to the continual staffing problems experienced at Woodhill this never came to proper fruition. Managing and staffing the separate centres as one overall unit complicated an already challenging task for management and staff.

Woodhill was initially envisaged, and emphasised to staff, as primarily a progressive system. But, as noted earlier, due to the non-cooperation and persistent challenges of a significant minority of prisoners, its role changed somewhat to incorporate the containment of prisoners considered too high a risk for ordinary location and for whom there was a need for a high degree of control. From April 1999 Woodhill was in effect officially operating a dual system: A and D wing *containing* prisoners and B and C wing *progressing* prisoners. Although this clarified their role for staff in the different wings, friction continued to exist over how in practice to fulfil two potentially contradictory functions within one system.

Effects of physical proximity at Woodhill

As all the centres at Woodhill were located in the same building, the disruptive behaviour of the prisoners on A and D wing who were not co-operating with the system had a far greater impact on the other centres than if they had been located in separate self-contained centres. Due to their close proximity, prisoners in the Restricted Regime Centre were able to exert pressure on prisoners in the Structured Regime Centre not to cooperate with the system. Some of the prisoners on B wing succumbed to this pressure and acted in a way that ensured their removal from B wing to A wing.

Similarly, when prisoners were actively protesting on either A or D wing (e.g. kicking/banging their cell doors or shouting abuse at staff), it was often the case that this sound (and in the case of the more prolonged dirty protests, the smell) travelled to B and C wings. At the very least, this kind of activity was a distraction to prisoners and staff in these centres and ultimately it undermined the progressive ethos and aspirations of the Structured Regime and the Programmes Intervention Centres.

Despite staff and management efforts the disruptive behaviour of the prisoners not co-operating with the system came to dominate both the overall atmosphere and running of all the centres at Woodhill. If these prisoners had been held in a centre that was physically separate from the other progressive centres their destructive influence on these centres could have been reduced considerably.

Variations in staffing arrangements

The manner in which Woodhill was staffed also contributed considerably to the difficulties experienced in its operations. There was one pool from which officers were drawn to staff the centres. It was originally intended that each centre would have dedicated staff working in them. This would provide continuity for staff and prisoners and offer greater potential for constructive working relationships to be established with prisoners. From its inception, however, Woodhill has never achieved the level of staffing for which it was originally profiled. Despite reprofiling and various attempts by staff and management to recruit more staff, Woodhill has struggled throughout its two years to staff the centres adequately.

Since staff were drawn from a main pool and were not attached to one of the centres full-time this meant that all the centres' regimes were undermined and continuity was disrupted by staff shortages. Although staff would be considered to be A wing, or B wing, staff, it was not official policy to ensure that staff always worked on the wing to which they were considered allocated. This meant that for a shift all the B wing staff, for example, may be available but due to shortages elsewhere in the system these staff were reallocated. While recognising the operational necessity for doing this, it was frustrating and undermining for those trying to manage their centre to have their allocated staff called away to meet short-falls elsewhere.

This method of staffing was further complicated by the fact that (since April 1999) A and D wings were primarily containing prisoners whilst B and C wings were progressing them. Thus, when staff covered the different centres they would find themselves having to operate in accordance with completely different principles and deal with the completely different responses. The more that staff were exposed to the very disruptive behaviour of the prisoners on D wing the harder it was for them to adapt to working with prisoners on the more open 'progressive' regimes of B and C wing.

CSC staff in Durham were able to form a good knowledge of their prisoners through working with them regularly and consistently, whereas Woodhill staff were only able to establish a much lower level of consistency and continuity with their prisoners as a result of their staffing difficulties. It is to the credit of staff that some positive prisoner-staff relationships nevertheless developed under such inauspicious circumstances.

Management structure

Although the two centres at Durham were managed by the same person they were always managed as separate entities. This meant that any problems experienced by one centre did not directly impinge upon the other. It also meant that staff identified strongly with their own centre, creating a supportive team spirit. Staff were aware of their role in each centre and what was expected of them.

Woodhill, in contrast, was managed as one overall unit rather than three separate centres; thus, the operational priorities and differences between the centres became blurred. Although each of the centres experienced their own problems and difficulties during the two years, it was the problems of A and D wings that were given overall priority by management. Other concerns, e.g. about the lack of regimes on B and C wings, were afforded less urgent priority as they did not have such a destabilising effect on the running of the CSCs as a whole.

Throughout the two year period the Woodhill centres experienced far more difficulties than the two centres located at Durham (or Hull, when the Intervention Centre was located there – apart from one serious hostage incident). Staff shortages undoubtedly contributed significantly to these problems since any initiatives implemented by management were always vulnerable to failure through the lack of staff to deliver the initiatives. Although the non-cooperative prisoners contributed in a major way to the difficulties experienced at Woodhill, the problems that Woodhill has faced cannot be solely linked to the fact that they managed the 'hard end' of the CSC population. It would appear that some responsibility for the problems must lie with the management structures in place at Woodhill.

The management structure at Woodhill made it very difficult to communicate adequately with staff and to ensure staff felt properly supported. For example weekly staff meetings were held at Woodhill, lasting approximately one hour. Within that hour the managers had to communicate to staff any issues of importance and in turn staff had to raise any concerns they had from their different areas of work. As noted above, each centre was likely to have different concerns regarding their regime and their prisoners. It was very difficult for all these issues to be communicated effectively and systems set up for addressing any lingering concerns during this one hour meeting.

In addition to the weekly general meeting, each centre also had a meeting with Psychology which lasted approximately one hour. These meetings were used mainly to review the prisoners in their centre, although issues such as conditioning or methods for managing problems that might arise from these reviews were also addressed. No member of staff above Senior Officer attended these meetings. Since there were essentially four centres this meant that each centre had a meeting with Psychology once a month. Although Psychology provided less formal input, three weeks was a considerable period of time for staff to operate without an opportunity to gather together and review issues.

In comparison, at Durham, in-depth staff meetings took place once a week with the centre being closed down for at least two hours to accommodate these meetings. This time was spent reviewing prisoners and raising any concerns regarding regimes and developing future plans for the centre. These meetings were also attended by the psychologsts (when in post), the psychiatric nurse, the Principal Officers (since their appointment), who often chaired them, and often by the centre manager. These meetings provided a high degree of both staff support and an avenue for constructive communication to take place. Lack of communication between management and staff and adequate provision of staff support remained areas of concern at Woodhill. The level of communication and support achieved at Durham was never accomplished at Woodhill during the time of our evaluation.

A similar difference was apparent in the use of staff briefings and debriefings. At Durham these sessions provided an important source of stress release and staff support in addition to an exchange of information between staff. They allowed staff an opportunity to share any difficulties that they had experienced, which in turn allowed them to put their experiences in perspective and thereby 'normalise' their working experience. Both the smaller groups of staff and the continuity in staffing appeared to promote a strong level of trust amongst staff which allowed staff to discuss their concerns openly and honestly.

In contrast, at Woodhill, these sessions were much more perfunctory in nature. There was less opportunity to discuss issues in detail because what was important to B wing was not necessarily of relevance to C wing. In addition, these sessions provided little, if any, of the emotional release and support that were achieved in the equivalent sessions at Durham. Although there were some attempts to increase the usefulness of these briefing sessions at Woodhill, such as ensuring Principal Officers were in attendance, a valuable source of staff support and stress release was missing.

4.   Staffing issues

Staffing structures, profiles and changes

All the CSCs experienced significant changes in their management structures and/or senior managers in the first two years of operation. Hull and Woodhill experienced a change of manager during the first year – Hull in May 1998 and Woodhill in January 1999. Durham experienced two changes of manager – in July 1999 and April 2000. Only the Hull Centre in its one year of operation retained its original staff profile.

Durham

Durham I wing was originally managed by a Governor 5, four Senior Officers and 22 officers. Owing to the promotion of the Governor 5 to Governor 4 this later changed to a Governor 4, one Principal Officer, three Senior Officers and 20 officers. This eventually became a Governor 4, Governor 5 (the Principal Officer taking promotion in situ) three Senior Officers and 22 officers.

In July 1999 the Governor 4 left the post, so that I wing and G wing were then managed by the Governor 5 still in post. Since there were no staffing changes related to these management structure changes the impact on the running of I wing was minimal. In November 1999 it was decided that a Governor 4 grade was more appropriate as CSC manager, and so a new Governor 4 was appointed to manage Durham I and G wings in April 2000. During the interim period, before this appointment, the Governor 5 continued to manage the centres and a Principal Officer was appointed to I wing. Since April 2000, I wing has been managed by a Governor 4, one Principal Officer, three Senior Officers and 22 officers.

When it first opened in May 1999, Durham G wing was staffed by a Governor 5, one Principal Officer, four Senior Officers and 20 officers and four Operational Support Grades (OSGs). As with I wing, G wing is now managed by the Governor 4. The original Principal Officer was later seconded to other work and was replaced in March 2000. Due to this change there was a period of time where G wing operated without a Principal Officer working there full-time.

Woodhill

Woodhill CSC was originally staffed by a Governor 4, three Principal Officers, 12 Senior Officers, and approximately 55 officers (Woodhill was originally profiled for 66 officers but with E wing only ever operating for a very short period there was never a full complement of staff at Woodhill) plus six Operational Support Grades (OSGs). In addition to the change of centre manager, Woodhill also experienced a high turnover of Principal Officers with five Principal Officers passing through the CSC in its first year. A number of these POs worked there for only a short time. This high turnover had an impact on the functioning of the CSCs and in particular staff's faith in management's commitment and ability to run the centre.

Towards the end of the first year, Woodhill's management structure was altered considerably by the introduction of a Governor 5 in addition to the Governor 4 centre manager. The number of Principal Officers was reduced to two. The number of Senior Officers remained at 12 and the number of officers required was profiled at 60.

The second year saw a change in the Governor 5 (January 2000) and one of the Principal Officers (May 1999). The new Principal Officer subsequently left the CSCs (and the Prison Service) in March 2000; so that Woodhill had to operate with only one Principal Officer until a replacement was eventually appointed in May 2000.

Staff turnover
Durham I wing

CSC Operating Standards recommended between two and three years' duty for prison officers working in the centres. Since some staff on Durham I wing had already served their 'tour of duty' (as many of the officers had been working on I wing prior to 1998, when it changed from a CRC to a CSC), some turnover of staff in the second year was inevitable. However, at the time of writing (May, 2000), just one Senior Officer and three officers had been replaced on I wing.

New staff who were being considered to work on I wing were interviewed by the CSC manager and spent an observation period in the centre before a decision on their suitability was made. (A similar process was used for selecting replacement staff for G wing.) This observation period allowed the officers to decide whether they felt they could work with the prisoners and in the environment of I wing. It also offered I wing management the opportunity to assess whether the officer would fit in with the ethos of the wing and the existing staff group.

I wing staff expressed concern about how staff rotation was managed. It was felt that moving too many officers off too quickly risked destabilising the centre. The interpersonal skills of staff and staff-prisoner relationships were seen to be the key to maintaining the stable and safe environment of I wing. It was important, therefore, to ensure new staff had become properly established and settled before moving any other officers out of the centre. Management shared this concern and there were no plans to move any more officers in the near future.

Many officers whose 'tour of duty' was coming to an end were reluctant to leave the centre. Staff enjoyed coming to work. There was a good team spirit and staff gained satisfaction from working constructively with the prisoners. Staff were confident in and proud of the work they did and were reluctant to leave what they considered to be a very good working environment. This positive endorsement and feedback by the staff who worked on I wing considerably eased staff recruitment to the centre.

Woodhill

This was in stark contrast to Woodhill. During the first year, five Principal Officers, four Senior Officers and 13 officers left the CSCs. During the second year, a Governor 5, two Principal Officers, five Senior Officers and 29 officers left the Woodhill Centres. Owing to the staff shortages many of the officers had to wait considerable periods before they could move from the CSCs.

Various avenues continued to be explored to address the staffing difficulties at Woodhill, including six month working periods, public interest transfers, receiving loaned staff from another House unit, etc. Staff recruitment was one of the issues examined at a CSC away day in April 2000, when it was decided to appoint a task force to address the problem. Unlike the CSCs at Durham (especially I wing), Woodhill CSCs were not seen as good working environments. The very negative image of the CSCs, which emerged initially from the assaults and dirty protests of the early days, still persisted. Little notice was taken of any of the positive work being done in the CSCs, but above all they were seen as dangerous and frustrating places in which to work.

The perceived lack of attraction of working in the CSCs at Woodhill meant that appointing volunteers became increasingly difficult. As a result, the process of being able to select staff carefully for the CSCs had to be virtually dispensed with. In March 2000 the senior management group considered a proposal to require staff to work mandatory periods in the CSC. However, the presence in the centres of staff who do not want to work there, or who are not suitable, creates an additional stressor in what is already a particularly stressful working environment.

Staff safety

The safety of staff was another key area of concern for officers working in the CSCs. As with so many of the issues at Woodhill, the staffing level played a role in this concern. Knowing they were not adequately staffed left staff feeling concerned about their safety, with the most volatile and dangerous behaviour occurring primarily on D wing. Despite the use of higher levels of protective equipment staff were still being periodically assaulted by prisoners. Serious concern was expressed about the effects that D wing's increasingly oppressive and hostile environment was having on both staff and prisoners. It became vital to find a way out of the deadlock that existed on D wing.

A definite hardening in the attitudes of staff towards the prisoners held on D wing occurred over the two year period of our evaluation. Whereas staff were originally keen to communicate with and encourage prisoners, even after the assaults and dirty protests of the early days, these sentiments largely disappeared in the second year. Understandably worn down by the continued challenges and violence, a degree of almost contempt towards these prisoners became apparent amongst staff. There is a strong risk that if the environment that exists on D wing is allowed to continue staff could well reach breaking point, and the professionalism of staff, which has generally been maintained to date, may well be undermined. In March 2000 an officer was suspended pending an investigation into an allegation of assault on a prisoner on D wing.

Other CSC management concerns at Woodhill

Management concerns at Woodhill, in addition to staffing and staff safety, have also focused on the excessive level of administrative work for management, the limited use made of middle managers by staff, and a perceived lack of local autonomy from headquarters.

Administration work for managers

Each prisoner had to have a monthly report prepared for the CSC Committee meeting, for which the managers had to oversee the considerable amount of paperwork required. In addition, as a result of the increasing number of judicial reviews by prisoners, prisoner allegations and the excessive use by some prisoners of the request/complaints system, the senior CSC managers found themselves dealing with an immense amount of paperwork, as well as responding to routine enquiries from solicitors and police. All this administrative work resulted in there being far less opportunity for them to spend time on the Centres, provide a visible presence and offer staff the support they needed.

Role of middle managers

A more serious problem was the fact that very few of the staff in the centres at Woodhill appeared to have confidence in their middle managers. This meant that the centre manager was drawn into often very basic decision making which should have been dealt with at a lower level of management. It seemed that staff felt they needed to clear most decisions by the centre's manager rather than through their own line managers. Rather than decisions being made at the level of officer, Senior Officer and Principal Officer, there was a tendency for all decisions to be pushed up to the top. Consequently, the centre manager was distracted from the overall direction and development of the centres, whilst leaving the staff feeling relatively powerless.

Local decision-making

This 'pushing-up' of decision-making appeared to be linked to the issue of how autonomous Woodhill management was in relation to Head Office (High Security Directorate). Although the lines of management between the CSCs and Head Office were made clearer when Woodhill and Durham were taken into the High Security estate, confusion still appeared to exist at Woodhill about where decisions were made in relation to the management of the Woodhill centres, in particular D wing prisoners. Given the high political and media profile of the CSCs, Woodhill management tended to be very cautious about the decisions they made and often sought advice from Head Office. This led to the perception by Woodhill management that their decisions could be, and often were, overruled by Head Office and also resulted in the position of local management being seen to be undermined in the eyes of the staff. Furthermore, this tendency for Woodhill management to seek advice reduced Head Office's confidence in them.

Thus, certainly in terms of staff and management perceptions, the operation of Woodhill centres appeared to be 'interfered' with in a way which seemed to be completely absent at Durham. This may have been linked to the more robust management approach which had been developed at Durham, where issues were thoroughly reviewed at a local level before being raised with Head Office (if that was required). Woodhill, on the other hand, had a far less robust approach to its management, a situation which was undoubtedly related to its perceived lack of autonomy from Head Office.

Staff concerns

Staffing levels and a failure to provide adequate regimes were undoubtedly the overwhelming concerns of staff at Woodhill during the first two years of operation. These two factors coloured all other aspects of working in the centres. The lack of consistency in regime provision undermined the ability of staff to work with prisoners beyond providing them with the basic requirements of showering, exrcise etc. Staff continued to feel that they were not adequately addressing their main objective of helping prisoners address the underlying causes of their disruptive behaviour. As in the first year, this inability to provide regimes as required at Woodhill had repercussions for the Activity Intervention Centre. Staff felt that some of the prisoners who progressed from Woodhill were not really ready to move as their level of behaviour was not appropriate for the centre. This meant that Durham staff had to work on improving the prisoners' behaviour before they started their own work of preparing them for a return to the mainstream.

The concerns of staff in the Durham centres were somewhat different to those at Woodhill, reflecting the differences in the way the centres had developed (see above). Since I wing experienced no staffing problems and had a well structured regime in place, staff concerns focused on enhancing the work they did with prisoners. Staff accepted that the majority of prisoners would be located on I wing for considerable periods of time and that it was, therefore, appropriate to develop more medium-term targets for the prisoners. While it was recognised that stabilising the prisoners' behaviour was important, once this was achieved staff should begin to challenge the prisoners more. This was an area that the newly appointed Principal Officer and Governor 4 were keen to develop and they were beginning to explore ways of incorporating more 'mainstream' targets for the prisoners that were linked to their overall sentence plan, or developing one where they did not exist, rather than focusing exclusively on their time in the CSCs.

In a similar vein, G wing staff expressed concern over what level of behaviour they were to expect from prisoners before they were ready to return to normal location. This concern took two slightly different forms. Some staff felt that the level of behaviour they expected from prisoners was much more than would be expected of them on normal location and perhaps as such they were preparing prisoners somewhat inappropriately for their return to normal location. Prisoners would not be expected to engage with staff to the level they did in CSCs nor would they be under the level of scrutiny that they were in the centres. Other staff felt that regardless of how prisoners behaved they would be returned to normal location due to pressure for the centre to appear successful. Staff expressed concern that their opinions about a prisoner's suitability or not for returning to normal location would be ignored. They worried that they would then be blamed for a prisoner's behaviour if they failed and more importantly to staff they worried that their colleagues would be put at risk if prisoners who were not ready were sent back to normal location.

Role of specialist and other staff

The other categories of staff who had a major role in the centres were psychologists and education staff. Although both probation and the chaplaincy were also involved with the centres this was generally to a lesser extent, typically on an 'as needed' basis. Since a large number of the prisoners in the centres were serving life sentences they did not feel they required the services of probation, although a number were seen by probation during their time in the centres, and some important individual work was being done by probation staff. Woodhill CSCs, however, were without their appointed probation officer for a considerable period in the second year due to long-term sick leave.

Provision of education

Five sessions of education, totalling 14 hours per week, were provided to the Woodhill Centres. Six hours of this was dedicated to C wing, in the form of cookery, food hygiene, health and safety and IT skills. Some individual tutoring was available to B, A and D wings, although education on A and D wing took the form of the provision of in-cell work for prisoners. Following the suspension of two of Woodhill education officers during the second year there was limited input to the CSCs due to the lack of available staff. On I wing Durham, 20 hours of education were provided over four days. Durham G wing were provided with 18 hours of education a week.

Education made a positive contribution to the regimes in all the centres and in some cases engaged prisoners who did not generally interact with other members of staff. However, there was a common concern expressed by education staff that education was merely a 'time filler' in the centres and was not properly linked to or integrated with any overall management plans for the prisoners. As a result, the potential developmental role of education was not fully utilised. More involvement of education staff in the overall management plans of prisoners would also encourage a better integration between education staff and centre staff, and hopefully reduce the feeling of isolation and lack of support experienced by some education staff currently working in the CSCs.

Psychological provision
Woodhill

Ten hours of psychological input were provided at Woodhill, shared between a senior psychologist, three higher and one basic grade psychologist. They carried out assessments of prisoners, following their arrival at the centres, and undertook individual work with prisoners mainly on B wing, but also on C wing. They provided the Enhanced Thinking Skills (ETS) programme on C wing, and compiled reports on prisoners at both the local level and for the CSC Selection Committee. Psychology also chaired the weekly prisoner review meetings, offered advice on regime provisions and were available for consultations with staff. The majority of the psychological work was focused on those prisoners located on B and C wings who wished to engage with the system and to progress. Although there was some contact with prisoners on A wing during the second year, in most cases this was with prisoners they had already commenced working with on B or C wing, but who had been downgraded to A wing as a result of their behaviour.

As in the first year, there was minimal involvement by Psychology staff with A and D wings in the second year, although some reports were prepared on the effects of the D wing regime on staff and prisoners. Since there had been virtually no Psychology involvement with D wing in the early days, the CSC staff became somewhat resistant to psychological input there later on. Their feeling was that since the psychologists had no contact with the prisoners and spent no time working on the wing they were not in a strong position to advise staff effectively.

Durham I wing
Since Durham I wing was the centre for highly disturbed prisoners, the psychological and psychiatric input was always intended to be higher than at the other CSCs. A psychiatric nurse provided four 3-hour sessions per week. This included individual work with prisoners, attendance at the weekly staff meeting and provision of training for staff relating to dealing with the prisoners on I wing. Early in its first year I wing had a consultant psychiatrist who attended management meetings and provided working papers to assist staff in their work with disturbed prisoners. For the majority of the time, however, the main input from a psychiatrist had been in the form of assessments. As the Operating Standards stipulated that I wing's psychiatrist should also provide education and awareness training for staff about symptoms of mental illness/disorder and the effects of medication, provide advice on the extremes of prisoner behaviour and give practical advice on the management of prisoners – as well as assist in the planning of the regime – it can be concluded that I wing was not providing the required level of psychiatric support.

Durham G wing
The Activity Intervention Centre (G wing) at Durham was intended to provide psychological assistance in the form of counselling and cognitive behaviour programmes for prisoners, and advice and support to management and staff in their dealings with individual prisoners. However, the Durham CSCs were without on site psychological provision for prisoners or staff

from June 1999. A principal psychologist was eventually appointed as Head of Psychology at Durham Prison in April 2000, but at the time of writing no psychologist had yet been appointed to provide dedicated psychological input to the centres themselves. During the autumn of 1999 psychological support had been contracted in, for one day a week, on a six months basis, whilst Durham attempted to hire psychological staff. Although this provision provided temporary relief it fell far short of providing the required psychological services for the centres at Durham as stipulated in the CSC Operating Standards.

Management of mentally ill and/or personality disordered CSC prisoners

The large number of mentally ill and personality disordered prisoners that the CSC system had to manage (see above) remained a serious cause for concern throughout the first two years. However, following the experiences of the first year, there was a greater awareness of this issue in the second year when some improvements were evident.

Slightly better communication and working relationships appeared to have been developed between the CSC system and the special hospitals system, although there could be long delays in carrying out assessments and awaiting transfer. In the case of one prisoner accepted for transfer, the assessing psychiatrist who had taken the decision left his post and another colleague replaced him. The prisoner's offer of a place was rescinded.

During the second year, five CSC prisoners were accepted by special hospitals. Of these, three prisoners were duly transferred, one was deselected to a healthcare centre for the interim period, and one prisoner was still waiting for transfer at Woodhill. The waiting time between a prisoner's assessment and the findings of that assessment, and the time between acceptance and actual transfer to a special hospital still caused considerable difficulty for the CSC system, particularly in Woodhill. One prisoner had a six months wait and two of the prisoners had a ten month wait before transfer out; another prisoner had been accepted by a special hospital after just three months in the CSC sytem, but was still awaiting transfer a further ten months later.

These delays created difficulties for the continued management of these particular prisoners within the centres. CSC staff were reluctant to start any new initiatives with a prisoner who had been assessed for a special hospital, and likewise some prisoners did not wish to become involved in any programme pending a decision on their assessment and/or transfer. Such prisoners were particularly difficult to handle in the open regime of I wing, where there was a strong emphasis on prisoner involvement, and where one prisoner's attitude could undermine the other prisoners' commitment.

Perhaps more importantly, these prisoners often displayed bizarre and unpredictable behaviour. They were considered too high a risk to be kept on the more open conditions of B wing and made such demands on staff resources that they seriously disturbed the centre's regime. Consequently, almost all the prisoners assessed as mentally ill ended up being managed either on the Restricted Regime Centre or the segregation unit. One prisoner was transferred from Durham I wing to the more controlled environment of Woodhill, where he was eventually managed on A wing. Whilst location on A or D wing may have reduced their risk factors to staff and prisoners (and in the case of some prisoners settled their behaviour to a degree) it restricted the level of psychological support they could expect to receive, and may not have been the most beneficial location when considering their clinical needs.

In view of the complex nature of the mental health needs of prisoners such as those being held in the CSC system (confirmed also by previous research relating to similar prisoners in the earlier CRC Units, e.g. Bottomley et al. 1994; Coid 1991), the seniority and level of clinical experience of the psychologists working in the Woodhill centres was surprisingly low, although they had been proactive in participating in specialist conferences and workshops, and in liaising with special hospital colleagues, in order to gain skills and assessment measures for use in the CSC context. Although trained in the normal range of prison work, the psychologists had not had specialised clinical experience in the management of psychiatrically disturbed offenders. Considering that these same psychologists both designed and presented the sessions dealing with 'Understanding Disruptive Behaviour' on the national CSC training course, and provided a high level of input into the assessment and management of prisoners in the CSCs, this limited level of relevant experience was inappropriate.

Psychological assessments

This limited experience of dealing with psychiatrically disturbed prisoners was reflected in the reports prepared by the psychologists. These reports generally contained little psychological understanding of the prisoners' emotional lives nor did they contain a detailed historical review of the individual's personality development and functioning. The absence of this information limited the potential usefulness of these reports in helping to identify, understand, and where possible, address the sources of the prisoners' behavioural difficulties.

It must be acknowledged, however, that the nature of the reports prepared by the psychologists were somewhat constricted by the requirements of the CSC system. To date, the CSC system has favoured reports that assess the risk a prisoner presents to others.

Therefore, psychologists' reports have emphasised analyses of prisoners' behaviour, adaptation to the unit and risk factors to the exclusion of clinical needs. The psychologists occasionally voiced concerns over some prisoners' clinical needs, for example at CSC Selection Committee meetings, but security and control within the CSC system tended to be given priority.

Prisoners' involvement with Psychology

Of the 36 prisoners managed by Woodhill in its second year, 16 of them undertook to work with Psychology. The remaining prisoners had either no contact with psychology (13) or only sporadic contact (7). Those prisoners who had infrequent contact with Psychology tended to have periods when they would engage with the system to some degree and then withdrew their co-operation when they experienced difficulties in maintaining an acceptable level of behaviour in the centres. Those prisoners who had no contact with Psychology were those located almost exclusively on A and D wings. Psychological input into A and D wings has remained minimal, although staff support and supervision has increased over the two years of operation and some work has taken place with individual prisoners located on A wing. In the majority of these cases, however, the work had already commenced on the Structured Regime Centre and continued when the prisoner had been downgraded as a result of his behaviour.

One of the major obstacles facing Psychology in their attempts to engage successfully with some of the CSC prisoners was the prisoners' perception of the role of psychologists within the CSC system (or, more generally, within the prison system as a whole). Some prisoners identified the psychologist's role as assisting managers in controlling and managing the prisoners, and even using confidential clinical material for this purpose. Psychologists were not considered to have any interest in assisting prisoners with their problems per se. Some prisoners felt it was inappropriate that working with a psychologist was intrinsically linked to progression through the system, and also resented the implication that there was 'something wrong with them'.

In addition to these attitudes, some prisoners had been offended by a newspaper article on Psychology in Woodhill CSCs, which gave them added reasons (in their minds) to be distrustful of the psychologists. Woodhill has made some attempts to address the issue of prisoners not co-operating with Psychology. Staff have encouraged prisoners to see the psychologists and an outside counsellor was made available to one prisoner in the hope that the counsellor could both help that prisoner with his problems and also encourage other prisoners to engage with Woodhill's psychologists.

Future role of psychologists

Practices need to be adopted that will regain the trust of these prisoners or at least allow prisoners to see some of the benefits that they could gain from co-operating with Psychology. It could be argued that, to date, Psychology staff have focused their work with prisoners on improving their institutional behaviour and have been less focused on concerns that prisoners may have about themselves and their situation. Adopting an approach that also focuses on the prisoners' clinical needs might encourage prisoners to be more cooperative. Similarly, separating sessions into those that address clinical needs and those that address prisoners institutional risks with different psychologists would also decrease prisoners' perception of psychologists as 'agents of control' for CSC managers.

Ways of increasing the psychological input onto A and D wing also need to be considered. Since Psychology has had virtually no contact with these prisoners, any assessments of prisoners on these two wings were based on wing files and previous psychological reports. As noted earlier, the quality of information found in prisoners' files was very variable, with psychological and psychiatric reports that were often repetitive and out-dated. Whilst recognising the difficulties of incorporating psychological input into these environments, the fact remains that those prisoners located on A and D wing share similar (or even more severe) psychological and psychiatric difficulties than those prisoners who are co-operating with the system and so it is vital to explore ways of assessing and addressing their needs.

The role that uniformed staff could play in both increasing prisoners' trust in psychology and in helping prisoners address their disruptive behaviour should not be overlooked. Durham I wing operated with minimal psychological input for over a year and yet successfully maintained the prisoners' behaviour in the centre. Successful use of interpersonal skills and modelling can be seen to have positively influenced some of the prisoners' behaviour. Increasing the social skills of prisoners, which in most cases are considerably under-developed, is one area in which staff could constructively influence prisoners. Allowing staff to take a more integrated role in helping prisoners address their behaviour offers the possibility of greater job satisfaction and a development of officer skills.

Finally, in this context, consideration needs to be given to increasing the input and degree of training officers receive regarding the nature of the prisoners' disruptive behaviour. Staff at all the centres have expressed both an interest in and need for increasing their knowledge in relation to the psychological and psychiatric aspects of the prisoners behaviour. The opportunities for this kind of interactive work are, however, more limited at Woodhill owing to the less interactive style of regimes and the more limited time out of cell, although with the introduction of basic group work on B wing there is a potential for staff input.

5. Effects of CSCs on prisoners

Prisoner progression and return to the mainstream

The underlying emphasis and objective of the CSC system throughout its first two years of operation was to progress prisoners through the system and return them to the mainstream as quickly and expeditiously as possible. Although the CSCs were designed as a progressive system with an ultimate aim, for the majority of prisoners, being 'to stabilise behaviour and prepare (prisoners) for a return to mainstream with minimum of disruption', no time limits have been stipulated in any of the CSC documentation as to how long this process should take.

This emphasis on 'quick progression' permeated decisions regarding the management of prisoners in the CSC, and was often a cause of concern and frustration amongst staff working in the CSCs. On many occasions staff felt that there was undue pressure to move prisoners through the system and that some prisoners were therefore moved on too quickly. It is not easy to document or discover where this notion of quick progression emerged from, as there is no mention of it in operating standards or official CSC documentation. It existed, nevertheless, and had a strong influence on the first two years of the system's operation.

If progression and return to the mainstream are used as the bench-marks against which to measure the effectiveness of the CSC system then it has achieved relatively little success with the prisoners it has managed to date. Between February 1998 and May 2000, twelve prisoners were transferred out of CSCs either to special hospitals (4) or normal location (8) – six in the first year, two in the second. Two other prisoners were deselected from the system.

Of the four prisoners transferred out to special hospitals, two have since been returned to the prison system and reselected into the CSC system. Both prisoners were moved out of the special hospitals following involvements in violent incidents. On return to the CSC system both prisoners have maintained relatively stable and co-operative behaviour.

Of the eight prisoners returned to normal location in mainstream prisons, three have been able to maintain an acceptable pattern of behaviour on their return and are still located where they were originally transferred. Four of the eight prisoners have been re-referred to the CSC system, of whom three have been reselected. One of the three prisoners re-selected was informed prior to his allocation of his acceptance into the Scottish Prison system, provided that he maintained a level of acceptable behaviour over a sustained period of time. He is in the process of maintaining a level of acceptable behaviour and so was not transferred into the CSC system. One prisoner at the time of his re-referral was no longer deemed to be at the 'same level of other CSC prisoners' and was to be managed by other methods. After disruptive behaviour, including assaulting segregation staff, he maintained an acceptable level of behaviour in normal location in a dispersal prison.

One other prisoner spent time in a segregation unit following disruptive behaviour on his return to normal location. It would appear that once the prisoner regained access to drugs his difficulties in behaving re-emerged. However, after a short time in the segregation unit he was returned to normal location where he was maintaining an acceptable level of behaviour. Finally, one prisoner was returned to I wing after a three month 'trial period' on normal location in a dispersal vulnerable prisoner wing. There were plans to relocate him to normal location again in the near future when a suitable location could be found.

In summary, therefore, two-thirds of the prisoners returned from CSCs to mainstream prisons, to date, failed to survive their departure from the centres, so that any beneficial effects or improvements in institutional behaviour derived from their time in CSCs was transient. There was a slightly higher rate of survival for prisoners who had been transferred to special hospitals, with two out of the four prisoners transferred remaining there. This relatively high survival rate, however, may have more to do with the different environments operating in special hospitals than any long-term effect of CSCs on prisoners per se.

Returning to the mainstream – prisoners' perceptions

Given the nature of the prisoners being managed by the CSC system one question that should be raised is whether quick progression back to normal location is a realistic objective for the system. As was noted in our Interim Report and the Inspectorate's Thematic Inspection of CSCs, many of the prisoners currently located in the system had developed deeply entrenched hostility and antagonism towards the prison system and prison authorities. They frequently cited brutal treatment by staff as the reason for their own violence and hostility. Many of the prisoners had stored up years of anger and resentment over their treatment by the prison system, whilst others expressed considerable fear and anxiety about returning to mainstream prisons which they had experienced as difficult and dangerous places in which to survive.

While it is impossible to confirm or deny the allegations made by prisoners of staff brutality, or their claims of the violent nature of dispersal prisons, it is clear that the prisoners' perceptions of situations in this manner have repercussions for how they behave in any given prison environment.

The majority of prisoners expressed little trust towards the prison system and regaining prisoners' trust and hence their co-operation is neither a straightforward or quick task. To address properly the underlying problems which give rise to the prisoners disruptive behaviour and hence increase the likelihood of them returning to, and remaining on, normal location would take considerably more specialist resources and time within the CSC system than has hitherto been considered practicable. Add to this the fact that a large number of prisoners would be deemed to be suffering from a personality disorder and/or various forms of mental illness (see below) and the complicated process of assisting them in addressing their disruptive behaviour becomes clearer.

Disciplinary records of CSC prisoners

In view of the past record of prison behaviour of the prisoners selected for the CSCs, another central question in assessing the beneficial effects of the centres must be the extent to which their patterns of violence and/or disruptive behaviour continues whilst they are in the CSC system. Addressing this question in a systematic way poses considerable methodological problems for the purpose of evaluation. Recording every incident of violence, threat or disruptive behaviour in each centre would require researchers to be present in the centres on a permanent basis, or alternatively to set up a system for staff to record all relevant incidents on a daily basis. In practice, we were not able or required to collect any such detailed documentation of the behaviour of prisoners in the centres.

Official data were available in the records of adjudications for offences against prison discipline, although the context and way in which formal disciplinary procedures of this kind are used in the centres are so different from that obtaining in the mainstream that such data are of questionable value for the purposes of detailed comparison between the past and present disciplinary records of the prisoners. In addition, adjudication data on prisoners prior to their selection into the system were difficult to collect and less than comprehensive. There was no way of verifying the completeness or accuracy of the records of prisoners' adjudications prior to selection to the CSC system. Despite these limitations, a rudimentary analysis of past and present disciplinary records of the prisoners was carried out. As far as possible prisoner adjudication records for at least two years prior to the CSCs opening and for the two years that the CSC system has been in operation were analysed.

Of the 46 prisoners whose adjudication records were analysed, 30 (65%) prisoners displayed a decrease in recorded adjudications after being located in the CSC system. Ten (22%) prisoners displayed a similar adjudication pattern to the one they had prior to entering the system. Six prisoners showed an increase in either overall adjudications or an increase in particular offences being committed.

Three prisoners committed assaults in the CSC system having had no prior record of such offences for the period 1995–1997 (all three were located on the Woodhill Restricted Regime Centre or in the segregation unit). Two prisoners showed increases in threatening and abusive behaviour and one prisoner showed a general increase in disciplinary offences. Four of these six prisoners had been located at Woodhill whilst the other two prisoners had been located in I wing and Woodhill, and in one case Durham G wing during the two years. It could, therefore, be suggested – tentatively, given the questionable reliability of the collected data – that allocation to the CSCs had some benefits in reducing the majority of the prisoners' disciplinary offences.

Behaviour of prisoners in the centres

Perhaps one of the most beneficial effects of the CSC system to date, and one that can be easily overlooked, is the way in which the system has allowed many prisoners to achieve some level of stability in their behaviour. In the past the main way of managing prisoners who have displayed disruptive behaviour of one form or another had been to move them, either to different wings in their host prison or to try them out in a different prison. This level of movement increased once a prisoner had been deemed disruptive enough to require allocation to the Continuous Assessment Scheme (CAS). Generally, once on CAS, both the prisoner's behaviour whilst in segregation units and the usually limited periods spent in any one segregation unit meant that any of the issues relating to his disruptive behaviour were left largely unaddressed. Any feelings of anger or frustration over their situation tended to be increased by the continual movement they experienced. For many of the CSC prisoners (at least 49% were ex-CAS prisoners) their periods of settled behaviour have been limited and the opportunity for prisoners and staff to address their disruptive behaviour severely curtailed.

Like the CRC units before them, the CSCs offered prisoners the opportunity to move away from the continual rounds of segregation units and provided them with a place removed from their previous problematic experiences to try and readdress their situation. Given the nature of the prisoners being managed – embittered, hostile, untrusting, disturbed – attempting to stabilise the behaviour of these prisoners should not be undervalued as an objective. It requires much of prisoners to move away from their positions of hostility and antagonism to a point where they might be more willing to look at their own behaviour and admit their own role in their predicament. Also given the nature of the prison environment and culture, especially in dispersal prisons there are many pressures operating on prisoners to maintain their disruptive behaviour (see below).

It requires considerable work and energy on the part of staff to gain any level of trust amongst such entrenched individuals, to reassure them and to tolerate prisoners' continual testing of that trust. In many cases, communication had completely broken down between the prisoners and staff, and attempting to rebuild relationships was a slow and difficult process.

It might be argued that, in the early days, CSC management was perhaps over-ambitious about what it could achieve with these prisoners and in what time-scale. However, it would appear that in the second year of operation a greater appreciation and understanding of the difficult and deep-seated nature of the prisoners' disruptive behaviour developed and was being acted upon.

Non-cooperation and protests

Although a majority of prisoners appear to have experienced varying degrees of stabilisation of their behaviour whilst in the CSCs, a small minority (eight prisoners) refused to co-operate with the system and sought actively to challenge it throughout much of the first two years. This group, therefore, cannot be said to have benefited from their allocation to the CSCs. In the case of seven of these prisoners, their behaviour deteriorated (often quite dramatically) following their allocation. These prisoners spent virtually all the time either in the Restricted Regime Centre or the segregation unit.

These prisoners originally protested against the CSC system because they saw their allocation there as inappropriate and unfair, or because they saw the system as unjust and a deliberate form of punishment, or both. The sparseness of the regimes at Woodhill, in particular A and D wings, in many cases added to the prisoners' hostility. Their protest took on a number of forms over the two years: dirty protests; legal challenges against allocation; continuous request/complaint applications; increasing levels of threatening and abusive behaviour towards staff (which is no longer restricted to prison officers but is directed at anyone entering in the case of D wing); assaults on staff; and allegations of misconduct and brutality against staff. As prisoner challenge was met with counter-challenge by staff and management so the negative and increasingly intimidating and dangerous behaviour of the prisoners increased. As a result, the segregation unit was unintentionally turned into a containment wing for those prisoners actively challenging the system.

The management of this small number of prisoners diverted a disproportionate amount of time and resources from the remaining centres and affected in a very negative way the overall atmosphere at Woodhill and the general morale of staff working there. Staff engagement and interaction with prisoners, a stated principle of the CSCs regimes, had been completely abandoned with these prisoners. By the time the fieldwork came to an end in March 2000 all prisoners on D wing were being unlocked with an SO and six officers in full Control and Restraint (C&R) equipment and in some cases shields.

Whilst in no way wishing to underestimate the extremely serious levels of intimidation and danger staff constantly faced from these prisoners, the ultimate result was a most oppressive environment for both staff and prisoners, with fewer and fewer options for prisoners to express themselves except through violence. Throughout the second year, CSC staff and management continued to struggle to find meaningful ways of engaging with these prisoners and to encourage them to consider progressing, or at the very least desist from, their overtly violent and disruptive behaviour.

The continued allocation and containment within the CSC system of this group of protesting prisoners, who had already been identified as disruptive and dangerous, appeared to be increasing their level of hostility. Concern has been expressed at Committee meetings regarding the potentially negative effects their continued presence on either the Restricted Regime Centre or the segregation unit might have in terms of their anger and potential expressions of this through violence. As long as these prisoners remain angry and embittered towards the system, it is highly unlikely that their behaviour will improve. However, there is an important principle at stake here – who will gain from this continued confrontation?

Given the level of sustained disruptive behaviour displayed by these prisoners during their time in the CSCs, it is easy to forget that four of these prisoners were maintaining relatively acceptable behaviour in the open conditions of the Hull CRC Unit (and also when it became a CSC), immediately prior to their transfer to Woodhill. It is also important to note that prior to their allocation to the system, the majority of these prisoners would have been managed in a segregation unit without requiring a SO and six officers in full C&R kit with shields to unlock them.

Whilst appreciating the Prison Service's concerns about not being seen to 'give in' to the prisoners who are challenging the system – and the message that this would send to other prisoners – one of the criteria for selection and exclusion/deselection (set out in Annex 1 of the CSC Operating Standards) states that a prisoner should be deselected if "the prisoner's behaviour can be dealt with more appropriately elsewhere in the prison system". Accordingly, if it seems that actually being in the CSC system may be increasing the risk factor of these prisoners (as has been identified to be the case for two prisoners), it would seem to be questionable management strategy to continue holding them within the CSC, and/or in the conditions under which they are currently being kept.

Psychiatric assessment of CSC prisoners

A key purpose of the research was to assess whether those selected for the CSCs were appropriately placed. This entailed conducting psychiatric assessments of the prisoners in each centre in order to see how they matched selection criteria and to assess whether any inmates showed signs of deterioration. The psychiatric interviews also contributed relevant observations in relation to three other aims of the research: first, assessing the extent to which the CSCs achieve key goals of safe containment, behavioural change and reintegration; secondly, assessing the extent to which centres alleviated problems of order and control; thirdly, drawing practical lessons for the prevention of disruptive behaviour and the identification of situations conducive to stability.

Interview sample

The aim was to seek to interview every prisoner in the CSCs, and subsequently to carry out follow-up assessments. The interviews were carried out between May 1999 and March 2000. In practice the logistical difficulties of conducting individual interviews, particularly at Woodhill, were substantial. Considerable amounts of scheduled interview time could not be used for that purpose despite careful pre-planning of times and arrangements. Frequently, at the appointed time interviews were not possible because of staffing pressures or other contingencies on the wings. Eventually it was not possible to carry out follow-up assessments, and the inmates who were interviewed were only seen at one point in time. This enabled the core aim to be achieved of obtaining a cross-sectional picture of psychiatric morbidity. We could also obtain a limited amount of retrospective information about past experience from the research interviews, but prospective follow-up of prisoners was not possible.

At the time of the interviews in Durham there were eleven prisoners in G and I wings. At the main period of interviewing in Woodhill, there were 24 prisoners in the CSC, but five of the seven inmates on D wing had been temporarily located in other dispersal prisons, leaving 19 potentially available for interview.

In all, interviews with 23 inmates were completed: nine at Durham, 14 at Woodhill, representing three quarters of those resident in the CSCs at the time of the interviews. Five prisoners declined to be interviewed (one in I wing, Durham, and two each in A and D wings at Woodhill). One of those who refused almost certainly suffered from a paranoid psychotic illness and he was awaiting transfer to a special hospital. The location of the prisoners at the point of interview is summarised in Table 5.1.

Table 5.1: **Location of prisoners at time of interview**

Location at Interview	Durham G Wing	Durham I Wing	Woodhill D Wing	Woodhill A Wing	Woodhill B Wing	Woodhill C Wing
Interviewed	3	6	0	2	5	7
Refused	0	1	2	2	0	0
Total in wing at time of interviewing	4	7	2 *	8	5	4 **

*   At the time that most interviews were conducted, five additional D wing prisoners had been transferred to high control cells in other dispersal prisons.

**   At the time that most interviews were conducted there were four prisoners in C wing, but interviews had been completed on earlier occasions with three other prisoners who had since left C wing.

Prisoners on A and D wings at Woodhill are under-represented for three reasons: they were more likely to refuse, interview access was more difficult, and some were temporarily located in high control cells in dispersal prisons because of the exceptional challenges they had posed.

Research instruments

A semi-structured interview schedule was developed to elicit information about the prisoners' background history (demographic details, educational and family background); psychiatric history (service utilisation); and prison history (including contact with medical services and history of deliberate self-harm). The interview schedule also contained a series of semi-structured questions about the prisoners' experience of the CSC regimes. This included questions on motivation, treatment, and psychological responses to solitary confinement.

Two structured diagnostic interview schedules were used to assess psychiatric diagnosis. The SADS-L (Schedule for Affective Disorders and Schizophrenia – Lifetime Version) (Spitzer and Endicott 1979) was used to obtain information on mental illness. In particular, the SADS-L enabled assessment of lifetime and current probable diagnoses of schizophrenia, affective disorders, anxiety, phobic and obsessive compulsive disorders. Personality disorder was assessed by the SCID-II (Structured Clinical Interview for DSM-IV Axis II Personality Disorders) (First et al 1997). The SCID II was also the preferred instrument in the recent ONS survey of the prevalence of psychiatric morbidity in the prison population (Singleton et al 1998).

To establish a diagnosis of personality disorder, there are general criteria that have to be met, and in addition there are specific criteria for particular kinds of personality disorder. The general criteria consist of evidence of an enduring pattern of personality traits that are inflexible, maladaptive and cause clinically significant distress or impairment in the individual's personal or occupational functioning. Personality disorders are disabling and this is manifest in different domains of the individual's life. The disorders are persistent and usually evident from the time of adolescence onwards.

The DSM-IV classification recognises three groups, or clusters, of specific personality disorders:

Cluster A disorders (paranoid, schizoid, schizo-typal);
Cluster B disorders (antisocial, borderline, histrionic, narcissistic);
Cluster C disorders (avoidant, dependent, obsessive compulsive).

Cluster A personality disorders are characterised by marked suspiciousness, distrust or detachment in interpersonal relationships, sometimes with oddness and eccentricity of affect and emotional expression. Cluster B personality disorders tend to be characterised by marked emotional instability, and Cluster C personalities by characteristics of anxiety and fearfulness.

The specific personality disorders in the DSM IV classification are summarised as follows:

Paranoid personality disorder is a pattern of distrust and suspiciousness such that others' motives are interpreted as malevolent.
Schizoid personality disorder is a pattern of detachment from social relationships and a restricted range of emotional expression.
Schizo-typal personality disorder is a pattern of acute discomfort in close relationships, cognitive or perceptual distortions and eccentricities of behaviour.
Anti-social personality disorder is a pattern of disregard for, and violation of, the rights of others.
Borderline personality disorder is a pattern of instability in interpersonal relationships, self-image and affect, and marked impulsivity.
Histrionic personality disorder is a pattern of excessive emotionality and attention seeking. Narcissistic personality disorder is a pattern of grandiosity, need for admiration and lack of empathy.
Avoidant personality disorder is a pattern of social inhibition, feelings of inadequacy, and hypersensitivity to a negative evaluation.

Dependent personality disorder is a pattern of submissive and clinging behaviour relating to an excessive need to be taken care of.

Obsessive compulsive personality disorder is a pattern of preoccupation with orderliness, perfection and control

(American Psychiatric Association 1994: 629)

Procedures

Each prisoner was approached to ascertain whether he would be willing to be interviewed. The nature and purpose of the study was explained. If consent was obtained, the prisoner was interviewed in private, but with staff observing from outside the interview room if necessary. In D wing at Woodhill interviews were to be in closed conditions. (An interview with one D wing prisoner was commenced but he subsequently declined to complete it and is therefore not included in the sample.) The duration of the interviews varied but averaged about two hours in total. They usually had to be conducted on two or more separate occasions because of time constraints on the wings.

At the end of each interview the prisoners' written consent was sought to examine their inmate medical records. There were sometimes difficulties of access to the IMRs in the Health Care Centres, as a result of which not all the records could be seen. Wing based files were also examined.

Psychiatric disorder
Personality disorder

Nearly two thirds of the prisoners interviewed (15 out of 23) met the criteria for a diagnosis of personality disorder. Of these 15 cases, one met the criteria for three types and three met the criteria for two types of personality disorder. The overall prevalence of personality disorder was similar to that described in the sentenced male population in the ONS study (Singleton et al. 1998). However, it should be borne in mind that the level of personality disorder amongst the interviewed CSC prisoners may be an underestimate for the whole CSC system because those who could not be interviewed were predominantly on A and D wings at Woodhill and were likely to have been more disturbed. It is also very important to stress that the SCID-II does not assess severity of personality disorder, but only the presence of personality disorder; i.e. whether a threshold for each diagnosis is met. The offending histories of the CSC prisoners, and the fact that a third have required admission to special hospitals in the past, indicates that it is highly likely that severity of personality disorder in the CSC population is greater than amongst other prisoners.

Antisocial personality disorder was the most common PD diagnosis (13 cases) followed by paranoid personality disorder (four cases). It should be noted that the SCID-II covers a wider range of personality abnormalities than the Psychopathy Checklist (PCL-R). In this population, the great majority of those with high PCL-R scores are likely to have antisocial, borderline or paranoid personality disorder diagnoses on SCID-II assessments (Stalenheim and von-Knorring 1996; Blackburn and Coid 1999). Blackburn and Coid (1999) also note that violent offenders in prison special units have considerable heterogeneity of personality pathology and their personality abnormalities are likely to be characterised by patterns of covarying traits rather than by single specific personality disorder types.

Table 5.2: *Personality disorder diagnoses*

Diagnosis	No with each type of disorder	%	Comparative prevalence in sentenced pop.
Paranoid PD	4	17%	20%
Schizoid PD	0		6%
Schizotypal PD	0		2%
Anti-social PD	13	57%	49%
Borderline PD	1		14%
Histrionic PD	0		2%
Narcissistic PD	0		7%
Avoidant PD	1		7%
Dependent PD	0		1%
Depressive PD	1		
Obsessive compulsive PD	1		10%
Anti-social only	9	39%	30%
Antisocial and other	4	17%	20%
Other only	2	9%	15%
Any personality disorder	15	65%	64%
Base	*23*		*210*

It was thought likely that one of the prisoners who did not meet these diagnostic criteria may have had Asperger's Syndrome (a disorder in the autistic spectrum characterised by impaired understanding of non-verbal communication and emotional expression).

Mental illness

In contrast, the prevalence of mental illness was high, and it appeared likely that, compared with the rest of the sentenced prison population, what distinguishes the CSC prisoners is not their rates of personality disorder but their high rates of mental illness and their co-occurrence of personality disorder and mental illness.

Table 5.3: *Mental illness diagnoses*

Diagnosis	No of prisoners who have had these conditions at any point in their lifetime	%	No of prisoners who have had these conditions whilst in the CSC	%
Schizophrenia	4	18%	3	13%
Other psychotic episodes	1			
Depressive disorder	9	39%	5	22%
Panic disorder	5	22%	1	
Generalised anxiety disorder	3	13%	3	13%
Obsessive/ compulsive disorder	1		1	
Alcohol abuse/ dependence	5	22%		
Drug abuse/ dependence	5	22%		
Base	*23*			

The principal conditions were major depressive disorder, schizophrenia, generalised anxiety disorder, panic disorder and alcohol or drug abuse/dependence. The data are summarised in Table 5.3, above. The table gives lifetime diagnoses and current diagnoses. 'Lifetime' means that the individual has had the relevant condition at some point in their lifetime. 'Current' means that they have had current symptoms of the condition whilst in the CSC system. The table shows that of those who have had histories of mental illness, most showed current symptoms of illness whilst in the CSCs.

Exact comparisons cannot be made with the findings of the ONS study because different instruments were used to measure rates of mental illness. However, it is of note that the ONS study found lower rates of current mental illness in the male sentenced population. The rate for psychotic disorder (in the last year) was 7 per cent; for depressive episode (in the last week) 8 per cent; and for generalised anxiety disorder (in the last week) 8 per cent (Singleton et al. 1998).

Only a minority of the CSC prisoners had no mental disorder (four cases), personality disorder alone (four cases) or mental illness alone (four cases). The remainder had combined diagnoses of mental illness and personality disorder. Tables 5.4 and 5.5 summarise the co-morbidity and the number of specific disorders amongst the interviewed CSC prisoners, and the prisoners' location at interview.

Table 5.4: Co-morbidity of personality disorder and mental illness

Diagnosis	No with each type of disorder (lifetime)	Prison wing	%
No disorder	4	A, B, B, C	13%
Antisocial PD only	3	B, C, C	13%
Drug/alcohol abuse only	1	C	
Personality disorder (any) only	4	B, C, C, I	17%
Mental illness (any) only	4	A, G, I	17%
PD + mental illness	11	B, B, C, C, C, G, G, I, I, I, I	48%
Base	*23*		

Table 5.5: Number of mental disorders

Number of diagnoses (lifetime)	Number of cases	Prison wing	%
None	4	A, B, B, C	17%
1	5	B, C, C, C, G	22%
2	7	A, B, B, C, G, I, I	30%
3	2	C, I	9%
4	0		
5	3	C, I, I	13%
6	1	I	
7	0		
8	1	G	

Background histories

A third of the interviewed prisoners had histories of being in local authority care, and a third had histories of special schooling. In addition, more than a third (10 cases) reported histories of physical or sexual abuse in childhood. Over half reported past contact with psychiatric services (excluding assessments for court reports) and over a third had previously been in special hospitals.

Table 5.6:   *Background social and psychiatric histories*

	Number ofcases	%
In local authority care	8	35%
Special schooling	8	35%
Juvenile court appearance (<17)	16	70%
Contact with psychiatric services	13	57%
Past admission to special hospital	10	43%
History of deliberate self-harm	13	57%
Base	23	

More than half reported histories of deliberate self-harm in the past. Two of the interviewed prisoners had made serious suicide attempts whilst on D wing at Woodhill, one by severely lacerating himself, one by trying to hang himself.

Segregation

It was not possible to obtain a full or representative picture of the experiences of those who had spent long periods of segregation for 23 hours a day on D wing at Woodhill. It was possible to interview four prisoners who had spent periods of time on D wing, two on dirty protests, in the past. They included the two prisoners who had made serious attempts to harm themselves. All reported adverse subjective experiences whilst in D wing.

One of these men, who had a probable history of schizophrenia, reported worsening fear, panic and hallucinations whilst on A and D wings, and he cut himself to try and get medical treatment.

The three other prisoners described becoming depressed in mood, withdrawn, and more angry and embittered, brooding on feelings of resentment. They described difficulty in thinking clearly and finding it hard to talk after long periods of isolation. Two reported weight loss and one thought he had some muscle wasting through lack of exercise. Two described blurred long distance vision. One described panic attacks. One developed paranoid ideas: for example if he heard laughter he believed those outside would come in and give him a beating. Their level of distress had been considerable. One, for example, observed:

"It makes you ill. It totally destroys you. It's very hard to describe how it makes you feel. ... We are the hard core of the prison system. They think we are hard and can cope with 23 hour bang-up, but we can't .."

Their strategies for passing the time included day dreaming (of their families), sleeping ("When you sleep you don't worry, do you?"), and trying to exercise. Their accounts suggest that a more detailed study of the psychological effects of these conditions is warranted.

Clinical services

The high rates of mental illness and co-morbid mental disorder amongst the CSC prisoners implies a need for strong supporting clinical services. Two developments currently add weight to this view. First, the Prison Service and NHS Executive report (1999) The Future Organisation of Prison Health Care emphasises that prison health care must be based on the principle of equivalence to the NHS. Secondly, the Prison Inspectorate's report (2000) Inspection of Close Supervision Centres August-September 1999 advises that the psychiatric profile of the CSC population indicates that the objectives of the system should include control and mental health support, and this would entail the management of the prisoners being better informed by clinical assessment.

Currently the level and extent of clinical support is deficient in a number of respects:

The CSCs were established without introducing new medical resources to the prisons, nor were specific arrangements made for psychiatric input at Woodhill. At the time of completing the field work, two years after the opening of the CSCs, there were plans at Woodhill to contract for an external forensic psychiatry contribution, and bids had been invited from several services (although none within close proximity to the prison).

The forensic psychologists provided base line assessments of prisoners on entry to the CSCs, and programmes of individual and group work on the enhanced wings, together with regular contributions to monthly and three monthly reviews. These contributions particularly focused on analyses of the prisoner's behaviour, adaption to the unit and risk factors. In cases where prisoners refused to see the psychologist the assessments were based on staff reports and records. As a matter of policy the psychologists did not have regular contact with prisoners on A and D wings at Woodhill: the opportunity for psychological help was primarily available for prisoners who could progress to the enhanced level of C wing. The assessments provided relatively little psychological and historical understanding of the prisoners' personalities and emotional lives.

The training of the forensic psychologists had been prison based without attachments in clinical service settings such as special hospitals. The psychologists themselves reported that whilst their training equipped them well to meet the normal range of work in the Prison Service, they had not had relevant training experience in the management of psychiatrically disturbed prisoners, including those with severe disorders of personality. This was evident in their assessment reports which were much less clinically comprehensive than would have been the case in a special hospital context. This state of affairs is problematic, given the lead role of the psychologists in the assessment and management of these prisoners.

At Woodhill there was no effective treatment partnership or team working with medical colleagues. Arrangements for clinical information sharing with their medical colleagues in the prison were out of keeping with health service norms. The psychologists did not have access to inmate medical records, including psychiatric reports and medication information on prisoners with whom they worked, because of an unduly narrow conception of medical confidentiality. (To obtain such information they were expected to obtain the written consent of the prisoner concerned, in the same way as non-clinical professionals.)

On the wings there was little working knowledge of the longitudinal histories of the prisoners. The wing files generally did not contain a full summary of the prisoners' histories and prison careers, of a kind that would inform psychological analysis, understanding of their behaviour, and recognition of the particular regimes and circumstances in which their behaviour has been stable or unstable. In some psychology assessments there was an attempt to identify periods of relatively improved stability with a view to identifying possible protective factors in relation to risk. However, substantially more could be done to analyse in a thorough and rigorous way available longitudinal information to identify the context and settings in which prisoners have shown periods of relative improvement and periods of relative deterioration. Such information would help provide a guide to regimes and individual management.

Some prisoners were reluctant to engage with psychologists because they perceived the psychologist's role as gathering information to be conveyed to management. There may be a case for reviewing whether the psychology input could have more of a distinctive clinical focus. It would be preferable if to a greater degree the role of psychology was perceived by prisoners (including those on A and D wings) as relevant and responsive to their psychological problems. Given the high prevalence of psychiatric psychopathology amongst the prisoners, and the relative lack of clinical training experience amongst the psychologists, it is particularly critical that their input is provided in partnership with psychiatry, and that there is a more multi-disciplinary and clinical approach to diagnosis, assessment and management. In the context of the recent proposals for the future management of dangerous people with severe personality disorder (Home Office/Department of Health 1999) substantive ways of joint working with the special hospitals, enabling consistency of clinical standards and more flexible transfers of prisoners, should be developed.

6. Impact of the CSC system on order and control in the dispersal system

One of the major objectives of the CSC system – like the combined CRC/CAS system before it – was to improve the level of order and control within the long-term prison system. In our series of visits to each of the dispersal prisons, in June 1999, we asked staff what effect (if any) in their view had the introduction of the new CSC system had upon the maintenance of order and control in their prison. Their responses to this question took various forms, but a high degree of consensus emerged.

Removal of CAS prisoners

There was general and widespread relief within dispersals that they no longer had to deal with prisoners on CAS. Interestingly, as we have seen (above), one of the consequences of the introduction of the CSCs was that almost half of the former CAS prisoners were subsequently returned to normal location where the vast majority seemed quite settled. However, an equally common response by staff at several dispersals was that, although a major aim and achievement of the CSC system had been the abolition of the CAS system, in practice there was still an unofficial CAS system operating, in the form of agreed 'swaps' between prisons and the continuation of informal 'lie-downs'. There will probably always be the need for measures of this sort, especially for prisoners who do not fit the official criteria for CSC referral/selection.

Order and control in dispersals

When we questioned staff in 1999 about the effect that they thought the introduction of the CSCs might have had upon the general level of order and control in dispersals, they found it virtually impossible to identify the particular contribution made by CSCs towards the general stability of their prisons during this initial period. In most cases they felt that there had been an overall reduction in the incidence of violence and serious incidents, with practically all reporting fewer cases of prisoners in long-term segregation, and with the population in segregation units seeing a steady (or sometimes quite dramatic) decline over the previous 12–18 months.

So many different initiatives have been introduced throughout the Prison Service during the past few years, intended and/or resulting in a greater degree of control over prisoners' behaviour (e.g. IEP, mandatory drug testing, volumetric control, tighter security measures etc.) that make it virtually impossible to calculate the independent impact of the new CSC system on the maintenance of order in the long-term prison estate. A welcome breathing space from a number of notorious trouble-makers had certainly been afforded, and the CAS system had been successfully wound down, but beyond that dispersal staff found it virtually impossible to arrive at any clear assessment of the precise effects of the CSC system.

In an attempt to discover some rather more objective and 'harder' evidence about the possible impact of CSCs on the level of serious incidents in dispersals, we sought relevant data from the Prison Service's incident recording system and 'Order and Control' matrix. The number of recorded acts of 'concerted indiscipline' and hostage taking are really too small for any scientifically sound conclusions to be reached. However, the trends do appear encouraging. For example, there was an average of three recorded incidents of hostage taking in dispersal prisons in each of the three years before the opening of CSCs, compared to just one incident in the last two years. Similarly, there was an annual average of 14 acts of concerted indiscipline in dispersals, 1995–1997, compared with an average of just 4.5 in 1998 and 1999.

As it happens, not many of the CSC prisoners had been frequently involved in concerted acts of indiscipline – but there were certainly one or two notorious hostage takers in the CSCs. A better indicator of the kind of serious incidents in which CSC prisoners are involved is the number of assaults on prisoners and prison officers or other staff. The average number of recorded assaults on prisoners and prison staff in dispersals for the three years before the introduction of CSCs was 33 per year; the average number of such assaults for the two years after the introduction of CSCs was 24. Curiously, perhaps, this reduction was not evident to the same extent across the dispersal estate. Thus, there was no statistically significant drop in prisoner/staff assaults during the last two years in Wakefield or Whitemoor, but there were significant decreases in Frankland, Full Sutton and Long Lartin – to the extent of an almost 50 per cent reduction of assaults in one prison.

There are other statistics that appear to show similar reductions in dangerous and disruptive behaviour during the past two years, such as for incidents of setting fire to prison property and, to a lesser extent, food refusal. All of these are consistent with the views expressed by dispersal staff that there seems to have been a general decrease in problems of order and control over the past two or three years. However, to move from that general agreement to claims that this is mainly due to the CSCs is not tenable. But whatever combination of policies and practices has helped to bring about greater order, safety and control in dispersals, this is a welcome trend, to which CSCs may justifiably claim to have made a small but essentially unmeasurable contribution.

Difficult prisoners and the role of segregation units

One of the most significant and encouraging features at virtually all the dispersal prisons we visited was the innovative ways in which they were addressing the behaviour of some of the difficult prisoners remaining in the dispersal system. Each prison was able to identify several current inmates who were causing them considerable trouble, and for many of whom there was no obvious solution to the question of their safe management.

At one dispersal prison, at the time of our first visit in June 1999, there were up to half a dozen prisoners in its segregation unit whom staff considered to be mentally ill; but as most of them fell outside the terms of the Mental Health Act there was really no other option available for them. A similar picture was found at another dispersal, where there were several difficult prisoners with psychiatric histories, who were reported as having virtually their own 'merry-go-round' of health care, segregation (basic) and normal location.

In most of these cases, the behaviour and/or personal characteristics of the prisoners did not meet the CSC selection criteria; often their diagnosed mental condition rendered them ineligible for consideration, or their sentence and previous disciplinary records were too short for them to be suitable for the timescale and scope of the current CSC system. In these circumstances, each prison was developing a variety of local strategies for managing difficult prisoners, with referral to CSCs being seen as very much a 'last resort', after everything else has been tried at the local level.

Several of the programmes being developed in dispersal segregation units, or other specially designated wings/units, involved multi-disciplinary team working, particularly with medical and psychology staff, as seemed appropriate. Indeed, in some cases there was evidence of good practices that the CSCs might wish to emulate. In this context, many common elements were apparent in the problems being faced by dispersals and CSCs in dealing with difficult prisoners. These included: the role of mental illness in the behaviour of many of the prisoners; the significance of pressure from other prisoners in their immediate living situation; and the increasingly flexible way in which material privileges were used by staff in dispersals as part of a realistic and effective strategy in the management of difficult prisoners.

7.

Cost effectiveness analysis

Cost data for the financial year 1999/2000, provided by the finance sections at Durham and Woodhill have been analysed in the context of the operational data collected during the fieldwork and reported in the preceding sections of this report. Prison Service accounting procedures, in common with those in many other parts of the public services, do not link expenditures with narrowly defined aspects of prison activity. Consequently, we were provided with the best available data, reported in Table 7.1, which identifies the total expenditure attributable to each of the CSC units at Durham and aggregate data for the four CSC wings at Woodhill. Although these data do not identify the costs of specific aspects of CSC activity, or permit a complete analysis of the cost characteristics of the CSCs, they are sufficient to identify the relative costs of the provision and benchmark the input of resources.

Table 7.1:   **CSC Accounting Costs 1999/2000**

	Durham I wing Total Costs (£ -000s)	Durham G wing Total Costs (£ -000s)	Woodhill CSC wings Total Costs (£ -000s)
Total staff costs	734	725	2090
% Running costs	95.9	94.4	98.8
Total running costs	766	768	2115

The costs reported in Table 7.1 exclude expenditures on utility services, which were not identified for all the units and so were excluded in order to maintain comparability. Similarly, no account was taken of the costs of higher level management and administrative inputs attributable to CSC units, which are accounted at prison level. Neither of these factors is a serious omission. Utility charges accounted for a very small proportion of costs (less than 0.5%) in the centres where they were identified. Management inputs were undoubtedly much larger, but the CSC units are small relative to the prisons in which they are located, moreover it is unlikely that these managerial inputs would have been avoided had the CSCs been located elsewhere.

Table 7.1 reveals the dominance of staff costs in the total running costs of the CSCs, with non-staff costs accounting for a very small proportion of the total (less than 5%). Having this in mind, it should be noted that the difficulty in recruiting and retaining staff at the Woodhill centres (see sections 3 & 4, above) has resulted in substantially smaller expenditures on staff than envisaged. Had the Woodhill centres operated throughout 1999/2000 with the planned staffing of 60 officers, total staff costs would have been in the order of £2.222 million and total operating costs in the order of £2.247 million. Thus, the overall cost of a fully staffed CSC system would be in the order of £3.781 million.

Average costs

The overall cost of the CSC system and the operating costs of the individual CSC units mask substantial variation in the average costs of the CSC regimes. Table 7.2 reports a range of average cost measures. The first measure is the cost per place, based on the certified normal accommodation (CNA) of the centres, which is one of the Prison Service's standard performance indicators. Cost per place is lowest in the Woodhill centres and greatest for the Activity Intervention Centre (G wing) at Durham, as was envisaged in the Spurr Report.

In practice, cost per place differed substantially from the level suggested by the standard performance indicator. Due to variations in the population of the centres, a variety of benchmark values might be considered. Table 7.2 reports values based on the maximum, average and minimum numbers accommodated in each centre over the period 12 months ending February 2000. Although the relative costs of the units remains unchanged, the cost differential between the Woodhill centres and those at Durham is substantially smaller, because Woodhill has to date operated below its maximum capacity.

Table 7.2:   CSC average costs 1999/2000

Cost per place	Durham I wing		Durham G wing		Woodhill CSC units Fully Staffed		Woodhill CSC units	
CNA	9	85,128	8	96,020	48	46,816	48	44,074
Maximum population	9	85,128	7	109,737	30	74,905	30	70,518
Average population	8	95,769	6	128,027	26	86,429	26	81,367
Minimum population	6	127,691	2	384,080	23	97,702	23	91,980

The cost per place data illustrate the difficulty in constructing and interpreting this statistic, due to its sensitivity to the population measure used. During the first year of operation cost per place in the CSCs was much higher due to lower occupancy rates, with the main exception being I wing at Durham which operated close to capacity throughout. Although no single measure is superior to the others, for comparative purposes the cost per place based on the average population of the unit provides a satisfactory guide. It is possible that this measure may overstate the cost per place for G wing, which for part of the period was in transition and occupancy rates were low. However, it should be noted that the Hull unit, which it replaced, also tended to operate slightly below its capacity.

Although there are no separate accounting data for the four CSC regimes at Woodhill, it is possible to infer the likely relative costs. The staffing profiles of the four regimes are very similar, with the implication that costs per place will largely reflect the numbers of prisoners accommodated in each unit. Education inputs are associated predominantly with B and C wings and their costs are attributed to only those wings. Table 7.3 presents estimates of the cost per place, based on the population data discussed in section 2 of this Report.

These estimates may overstate the costs of operating B wing, to the extent that a slightly lower staffing level is projected, than that used in the construction of Table 7.3. Moreover, the costs of the four wings at Woodhill will, in practice, have been different from those indicated, because the units have not, to date, operated with the full complement of officer grade staff.

Table 7.3:   Woodhill units: estimated average costs 1999/2000

Unit analysis	Woodhill A wing		Woodhill B wing		Woodhill C wing		Woodhill D wing	
CNA	12	46,288	12	46,808	16	35,106	8	69,431
Maximum population	9	61,717	10	56,169	9	62,410	7	79,350
Average population	7	79,350	7	80,242	6	93,615	5	111,090
Minimum population	6	92,575	5	112,338	4	140,423	3	185,150

None of the Woodhill units has operated at its maximum capacity and at times prisoner numbers have been small, implying much greater cost per place. Bearing in mind the caution outlined above, it is difficult to put forward a single measure which is representative across the wings. In addition, the fieldwork revealed that some regimes proved difficult to operate even though prisoner numbers have been well below capacity. B wing, in particular, at one period proved difficult to run when there were more than eight prisoners in the centre. The use of full C&R procedures when moving prisoners on D wing, similarly, made operation difficult, even though populations have been below maximum capacity.

A noteworthy feature of the data is that C wing has in practice operated well below its capacity, with the result that cost per place (average population) is closer to that of the Durham units than the CNA-based index would suggest. For comparative purposes, cost per place based on the average population was broadly representative, for most wings. The main exception to this was B wing, where the costs may be overstated, for the reasons noted above. Taking account of the distribution of prisoners among the wings, a central estimate of the cost of a place in the CSC system in its second year of operation was in the order of £95k. However, as the previous analysis shows, this masks considerable variation across the units.

Despite their limitations, the cost per place indicators are valuable in that they can be compared with the estimated costs of alternatives to accommodation within the CSC system. As was noted in the Interim Report, the relevant consideration for cost effectiveness analysis is the additional cost of placing a prisoner in the CSC system, rather than in relevant alternative accommodation. Evidence summarised elsewhere in the report, indicates that the population of the CSCs is diverse and the nature of alternative accommodation is a complex issue. Prisoners entering the system had in almost all cases formerly been held in segregation, usually in a dispersal prison, although a few entered (or re-entered) having spent some time in a secure hospital. Some prisoners leaving the CSC system have returned to normal accommodation in the dispersal estate, some have been accepted by one of the special hospitals and others will require long-term containment in non-standard accommodation.

For those (few) CSC prisoners who might otherwise be accommodated within the ordinary dispersal system, the comparable annual costs would be in the order of £40k. This implies additional costs for a CSC place ranging from around £40k (Woodhill A & B wings) to £88k (Durham G wing), with a central value of £55k. For many prisoners the alternative accommodation would be some form of segregation, for which the costs will typically be greater and the additional cost correspondingly smaller. Unfortunately, for the reasons outlined above, these costs cannot be established from the available accounting data.

Although not directly comparable with the CSC system, because of their admission criteria, annual cost per place estimates for the special hospitals can be constructed using published data (National Health Service (England) Summarised Accounts 1998–99, Department of Health and IHSM Health and Social Services Year Book 1998–99). Estimated cost per place ranges from £101k to £123k per place, with a central value (weighted average) of £110k per place.

Marginal cost

For many managerial decisions, the relevant cost concept is the marginal cost, i.e. the change in cost associated with the change in the activity level, rather than average cost. However, due to the regime based staffing of the units and the predominance of staff costs in total costs, the marginal (accounting) costs of accommodating a prisoner in a CSC unit operating at below full capacity are constant and close to zero. Consequently, marginal accounting costs offer little assistance in decision making.

Economic Costs

Accounting costs reflect only the financial transactions associated with the running of the CSCs, whereas the concept of economic costs is a broader one, taking into account effects which are not reflected in monetary transactions and encompassing the concept of external costs. The fieldwork reported in the previous sections identifies a range of factors which imply that economic costs may be substantially in excess of accounting costs. Some of these economic costs arise from the process of change and may be transitory. However, our evidence suggests that some have been persistent factors, to which a value should be attached.

Although each of the CSC wings has typically operated at less than full capacity (see 7.9) in practice the Woodhill regimes, in particular, have proved difficult to operate, with the implication that economic costs exceed accounting costs at population levels less than full capacity. The economic costs cannot easily be determined directly, however an approximation can be obtained by establishing the effective capacity of the unit – the number of places which can be provided and supported effectively, which may then be used in computing the associated cost per place. As we have already noted, B wing was at one time difficult to operate with more than eight prisoners. However, subsequent consideration of the operation of the Woodhill centres, including discussion at the CSC away days, suggests that the effective capacity of A, B and C wings is ten places. Table 7.4 reports the associated economic and accounting costs where, as in Table 7.3, B wing costs may be overstated.

Table 7.4: Woodhill units: Eetimated economic and accounting average costs 1999/2000

Unit Analysis	Woodhill A Wing		Woodhill B Wing		Woodhill C Wing	
CNA (Accounting cost)	12	46,288	12	46,808	16	35,106
Effective capacity (economic cost)	10	55,545	10	56,169	10	56,169

A further but less obvious factor in economic costs is suggested by CSC Selection Committee decisions concerning the movement of prisoners between the CSC regimes. In a small but significant number of cases, the progression of prisoners has been inhibited (or, in fewer cases, artificially accelerated) due to the perceived risk factor arising from personal conflicts between prisoners. Here the implication is that the marginal economic cost of accommodating a prisoner in a unit will often have both prisoner and context specific dimensions, which drive up the marginal economic cost, even though (with spaces unoccupied) marginal accounting costs are constant and close to zero. Moreover, a restriction on the mobility of one prisoner will often have additional external costs, due to the adverse implications for the movement of others. Thus, although there may be sufficient physical and effective capacity to allow movement, the marginal economic cost of a place typically rises as occupation rates increase to the point where some movement may be prohibited. The contribution to economic costs, implied by decisions on prisoner movements, cannot be identified directly and in any event is likely to vary over time. Nevertheless, recognition of these economic costs is important, in that they signal that investment in additional capacity may be justified.

A further operational difficulty, mainly experienced in Woodhill, has been the problem of recruiting and retaining staff, which may be due in part to the stress caused by the working environment. In a system based on the maintenance of specified regimes, the shortage of staff raises the economic cost further. Operationally the Prison Service is highly adaptive and the operation of a unit is typically maintained through a process of adaptation within the prison, with the result that the impact of staff shortages and consequent disruption are internalised. Thus, for example, severe staff shortages in the CSCs have been addressed by temporarily assigning staff who normally work in other parts of the main prison. Such re-assignments go unrecorded in accounting data because, under the current budgetary arrangements, the units are located within the same accounting cost centre and there is no need for a transfer payment to reflect the switching of resources.

Although the allocation of the available resources to those units where the problems are most acute is a rational process, capable of minimising the economic cost of the shortage of staff, adaptation will typically have a net economic cost. Economic costs exceed accounting costs by an amount representing the value of the work not being done by the substitute officer elsewhere in the prison, plus the value of any qualitative difference between the work of a specifically trained CSC officer and the substitute. Such costs are again not easily quantified, not least because they vary from case to case, due to the nature of the adaptations made.

Because the delivery of specific prison regimes cannot be specified precisely or closely monitored, minor variation is relatively easily achieved. Thus, in some circumstances the best response to staff shortages will be to use the available staff and deliver the regime as well as is possible under the prevailing circumstances. Due to staffing problems, the Woodhill CSC units have at times not operated to the specified regimes. Deviations have included, among others, the lack of constructive activity for prisoners on C wing, lower than projected levels of staff-prisoner interaction and, in more extreme cases, cut backs in prisoner association time. In these examples, the economic cost of the regimes having not operated as intended is borne by the prisoners in the form of lost benefits. Such economic costs are hard to measure because there is no mechanism for prisoners to demonstrate the value of the shortfall in the regime. However, they may be substantial and if ignored may lead to yet greater economic costs. For example, to the extent that prisoners become harder to manage as a consequence of the shortfalls, there may as a result be a greater degree of stress on those officers who are able to work, making work in the CSCs less attractive to potential officers, and thereby exacerbating the staffing problem.

Whether (an approximation to) the economic costs should be included in an evaluation of cost effectiveness is a difficult issue. Apart from the fact that economic costs relate to non-market transactions and so have no explicit monetary value, making them hard to quantify, in some cases the costs are a reflection of a process of adjustment and are relatively shortlived. That the economic costs of operating the CSCs, over the last two years, has exceeded the accounting costs is apparent from the fieldwork evidence. However, the system has been in a state of flux throughout the period and the costs may yet prove transitory and could be set aside. If, on the other hand, conditions are not expected to change, the full economic costs should be taken into account.

In the event that the full economic costs are to be considered, they might be approximated, as above, by determining the (lower) sustainable population at which each of the centres could operate effectively, given the staff and resources available, without incurring additional economic costs. The cost per place might then be calculated using the sustainable population of the centre, providing an approximation to the economic cost per place. Similarly, the marginal economic cost of a place in a centre should be regarded as positive and increasing at an increasing rate as prisoner numbers rise beyond the sustainable population.

Evaluation of effectiveness

The Spurr Report, which established the framework of the system of CSCs, identified the main attractions of the change as:

The removal of disruptive prisoners from ordinary segregation units
The deterrent effects on other prisoners
Coherence with an incentives based strategy
Provision of a stable environment for disruptive prisoners

However, unlike other aspects of the strategy and its implementation, which were addressed in detail, the expected benefits of the system were not identified explicitly. Benefits are anticipated to the extent that the new system was perceived as an improvement on what had gone before. However, it is unclear what the nature of the anticipated benefits were, how and where they were expected to arise, or the time-scale in which they might be realised.

The economic benefits from the changes anticipated by Spurr are second order effects, in the sense that the tangible benefits of adopting the CSC system are dependent on the adaptations made in response to that change. So, for example, the removal of disruptive prisoners was expected to free up 20 segregation places in the dispersal estate. However, no consideration was given to what resources would be released, how that might generate an economic benefit, or how the benefit might be detected. Similarly, although the deterrent effect of a strict regime on other prisoners and the benefits in handling difficult prisoners was asserted, no consideration was given to the mechanisms by which this might be brought about and in turn, how benefits might be realised. Thus, there was unlikely to be any immediate impact effect on economic benefits and, in the absence of mechanisms to monitor and give direction to responsive change, a significant prospect that the potential benefits would not be fully realised.

If, as is likely, the CSCs have created a potential benefit, in an environment where prison managers exercise discretion in adapting to change, the lack of focus in redirecting the resources freed up will almost certainly have resulted in benefits being widely diffused. In many cases prison managers might simply have been able to make minor changes improving the delivery of their existing regimes. An inevitable consequence of such adaptation is that there is no focus of the sort required for a comprehensive 'before' and 'after' comparison. Thus, taken together, the circumstances under which the CSC system was established pose considerable problems in both the identification and evaluation of the economic benefits resulting from the change. The change, in effect, concentrated the (acknowledged) high costs of handling a difficult group of prisoners in the CSC system, while few of the benefits (which may collectively be substantial) are realised within the CSCs, or are unambiguously attributable (or attributed) to them.

Possibly the most influential factor motivating the development of the CSCs was a sense that the system would improve order and control in both the CSCs and in the long term prison estate. Thus, the major source of anticipated benefits is the reduction in disruptive behaviour and the attendant costs. A framework for the valuation of these changes was outlined in the Interim Report, which emphasised the concept of expected value, in which the effect of the CSC system is reflected in the change in the probability of each class of disruptive effects. Drawing on the argument in sections 3 and 6, we may conclude that there has been no clear benefit through improved prisoner behaviour in the CSCs. Although the incidence of some forms of disruption appear to have declined other, relatively unusual forms, such as dirty protests and concerted legal actions, have markedly increased. Changes in the incidence of disruption in the long term prison estate appear more positive, however the available data do not enable the identification of the effects which are attributable to the CSCs or their value.

Observations made in the fieldwork identified several ways in which the CSCs may have had a beneficial effect, both within the system and beyond. Although the main benefits might be expected to accrue in the general long-term prison system, some economic benefits have been realised within the CSC system, particularly in the management of prisoners. There is a benefit to some prisoners, to the extent that the CSCs have provided a less pressured environment than long term accommodation in ordinary segregation units. In a small number of cases, prisoners' mental health and personality problems have also become better understood and have been taken into account in planning their progression. However, there is no obvious way in which a monetary value might be attached to such psychological benefits, or to determine whether such benefits have been fully realised. Equally, there is a group of prisoners alienated by the strict regimes, for whom the psychological effects are clearly negative. Thus, the balance of effects is indeterminate.

A less obvious benefit of the CSC system, revealed by the fieldwork, is that some dispersal prisons have developed new activities within their existing regimes and procedures, particularly in handling disruptive prisoners. Such innovation might not have been possible had the CSCs not been established and CAS ended. Although it appears that the effect has been to reduce the number of incidents in the dispersal estate, it is unlikely that the resources made available for such work with prisoners will be optimal.

Another way in which the CSC system has produced tangible benefits is through the reduction in the movement of (typically high risk) prisoners between segregation units within the dispersal estate, which characterised the operation of CAS regime. Although some prisoners under the CAS regime made few moves, others were moved to another unit as frequently as the system allowed. Thus, on average, a prisoner under the CAS regime was moved six times during a year. In the first two years of operation, the CSCs accommodated at least 25 prisoners who were formerly held under the CAS. The CSCs have not entirely eliminated the movement of prisoners between units and some CSC prisoners have been transferred to HCCs for 'lie downs'. Over the two year period (Feb 1998–Feb 2000) there were 26 transfers of CSC prisoners for these purposes, implying 52 movements, compared with anticipated movements of these prisoners under a continuing CAS regime, estimated at 300 over the same period. If account is taken of the reduction in the average distance travelled and time taken up in prisoner movements, under the CSC regime the benefits from the reduced costs of movement are in the order of £97.1k. If, as might be anticipated, prisoners transferred to the CSCs were among those transferred more frequently than average, this may be regarded as a lower bound estimate.

Insofar as the CSC system has had the anticipated effect of enabling the return of disruptive prisoners to long-term accommodation in the dispersal estate, there is the prospect of long term savings amounting to the annual cost saving over the remaining years of the prisoner's sentence. However, to date only four prisoners have made the transition anticipated. The value of these benefits cannot be established with any precision from the available data. Assuming that, on average, these prisoners are expected to remain in ordinary accommodation, rather than long term segregation, for a period of 20 years and taking the incremental cost per place to be £55k per year, would imply savings (at current value) in the order of £400k.

Cost effectiveness

From the limited information and evidence available at this early stage in their development, the accounting costs of managing disruptive prisoners in the CSC system are substantially greater than the tangible and quantifiable benefits. However, as noted above, in implementing the CSC system the Prison Service, in effect, focused the costs of this aspect of its work, making them more identifiable. In practice, the accounting costs almost certainly understate the economic costs of the system, due mainly to unanticipated problems in implementing the regimes and the effects of the subsequent process of adaptation. Whether the economic costs of the CSCs will continue to exceed the accounting costs rests to a substantial degree on the strategy adopted by the Prison Service in developing the system.

In marked contrast with identification of costs, the benefits of the CSCs, which in any event are much less easily defined, were also left relatively unfocused. Drawing on the fieldwork findings, we have identified several sources of actual and potential benefits for the long term prison system, that may be attributed to the CSC system. However, some of the benefits are intangible and most are not readily quantifiable. Some of these benefits may be more easily quantified in the future, when the effects of the system on prisoner behaviour can be assessed in a longer term perspective, but it is unlikely that the data available will be sufficient to sustain a comprehensive assessment.

8.   The CSCs: incentives and progression

CSCs will provide a co-ordinated range of regimes to manage seriously disruptive prisoners. The regimes aim to facilitate change and encourage improved behaviour. CSCs will operate within a framework of incentives and earned privileges. Enhanced level privileges will not be available within the CSC system.

(Principle 5 Operating Standards)

A prisoner's time in the Centre will be determined by individual assessment against targets, personalised compact and general regime compliance.

(Principle 4.9, Operating Standards)

The CSCs were established to operate as part of a national management strategy which aimed "to secure the return of problematic or disruptive prisoners to a settled and acceptable pattern of institutional behaviour". To accommodate this aim a system of staged centres was established which offered incentives for co-operative behaviour, with progressively more privileges at each level.

A major difficulty in assessing whether the centres constituted an integrated progressive system is the fact that for most of the first two years the regimes in the Woodhill Centres did not operate as stipulated in the Operating Standards. Virtually no constructive activities or behaviour programmes took place on the Structured Regime Centre (B wing) at Woodhill, and only very limited activities and programmes took place on the Programmes Intervention Centre (C wing).

This resulted in considerable imbalance and discontinuity between the Woodhill centres and the Activity Intervention Centre at Durham (G wing, and previously Hull A wing), so that the system lacked any real progressive coherence. It is impossible to judge whether the CSC system would have been more coherent and integrated if the Structured Regime and Programme Intervention Centres had functioned more effectively as intended in the first two years. In order to appreciate some of the difficulties experienced by the CSC system, particularly the Woodhill centres, it is necessary to examine the framework and philosophy from which the centres evolved. (For a more detailed analysis of the origins and development of the CSC system and the various issues discussed here, see Appendix 1, by our Project Consultant, Alison Liebling, upon which this section draws heavily.)

Origins and aims of the 'progressive' system

The Spurr Report (Prison Service 1996) recommended that the hard-core of seriously disruptive prisoners should be managed in a co-ordinated system of five Close Supervision Units (subsequently designated Centres) with graded regimes which would replace the existing CRC Units and the Continuous Assessment Scheme (CAS) which had grown up around it.

The intended aim of the CSC system was "explicitly to manage disruptive prisoners in conditions of safety for staff and other prisoners and to provide encouragement and opportunity for them to change their behaviour. It is explicitly not aiming to punish" (Prison Service 1996:66). Its core operating principles included a framework of incentives and earned privileges, formally published procedures and reasons for allocation, a co-ordinated set of regimes, no consent of prisoners required, formal assessment and review, active staff engagement, avoidance of 'drift' and 'conditioning' and external audit. Prisoners would begin in a structured regime and would be able to progress (to one of a range of intervention units) or regress (to the restricted regime) depending on their behaviour.

This scheme was intended to provide clear incentives for progression with an additional number of high control cells for those prisoners whose behaviour became so exceptionally dangerous that they threatened the operation of the centres. Prisoners would begin in the structured regime (unless exceptionally dangerous) and then progress either upwards or downwards, according to their behaviour. The CSC system offered more flexibility than the previous CRC units as disruptive behaviour in the more open intervention units could result in a return to a structured regime rather than deselection and return to the mainstream.

The Spurr Report had devised a model that was intended to include and manage the most disruptive, uncooperative and subversive prisoners. It was deliberately intended to be 'more robust' than the liberal but arguably only partially effective CRC system and to cater for the most difficult cases.

Implementation of the Spurr Report: from policy to practice

As is the case with any major report or inquiry, the core concern (or 'gist' – to use Liebling' term; see Appendix 1) has to be officially endorsed and then translated into policy and practice. In the case of the Spurr Report its core concern or message was interpreted as being about prisoner 'progression'. Accordingly, the Report was translated into a set of recommendations aimed at moving intractable prisoners upwards though the system and then to return them safely back to mainstream conditions. The manner in which the Spurr Report was interpreted and translated into practice highlights a number of the key concerns regarding the progressive nature of the CSC system and its applicability to the group of difficult prisoners it was designed to manage.

The level of material privileges

One of the key principles of the Spurr Report was that material conditions in the mainstream prison system should always look more attractive to prisoners, so that the standard of privileges in the CSC system should never be permitted to reach the level achievable in enhanced dispersal conditions. Therefore, the maximum level of privileges in the CSC system had to be lower than that of the maximum allowed in dispersal prisons. However, since each stage of the CSC system had to offer progressively more privileges, the minimal level was set at a low basic standard, even in comparison with some dispersal segregation units.

In practice, however, selection to the CSCs and transfer to the Structured Regime Centre at Woodhill (a key location, as prisoners' reactions and behaviour here determined their future location within the system) often resulted in a substantial lowering of the material privileges available to prisoners. Whatever the original intention, the Structured Regime of B wing was regarded as punitive by CSC prisoners and the level of privilege entitlement was regarded by them as severely restricted. Furthermore, staff interpretation of prisoners' privilege entitlement was, in the early days of the operation of the system, even more restrictive than was originally intended by the Spurr Report.

Considerable difficulties were experienced in convincing prisoners that their restrictive living conditions were justified. Prisoners (and to some extent staff) found it difficult to disentangle low levels of material provision from punishment. The considerable lowering of their material conditions led to a significant number of prisoners rebelling against the system and refusing to cooperate.

Very few prisoners who experienced Woodhill, particularly in the first year, perceived it to be a progressive system offering them an opportunity to address their difficulties and move on. The impact of the low level of material privileges initially available at Woodhill on prisoner behaviour should not be underestimated. In this context, it should be noted that since the increase in basic privileges virtually no new CSC referrals have reacted to the system in the negative and confrontational way in which the first prisoners did.

The restricted regime

The Spurr Report argued for a strict regime unit on the grounds that the relatively open CRC regimes had in practice required prisoners' consent and thereby had effectively excluded prisoners with a record of especially disruptive behaviour. In proposing the CSC system, it was claimed that a strict regime would provide a deterrent, the system was compatible with the recently introduced incentive and earned privilege strategy, it would link progress more clearly to prisoners' behaviour, and would provide an opportunity for assessment (Prison Service 1996; and see Appendix 1, below).

There were, however, concerns that such a regime (and the prisoners subjected to it) would become negatively labelled, that some prisoners would regard admission as a 'badge of honour', that violent and unstable behaviour would be exacerbated, that prisoners would remain for long periods, that there would be high levels of pressure and stress for staff, and that litigation would ensue (Prison Service 1996, 15–16). All of these concerns were to prove well founded.

Prisoners' reactions

Since their inception, the Restricted Regime Centre (A wing) and D wing – after its function changed from segregation unit to that of a long-term control and containment unit (as a result of prisoners challenging the system) – were perceived by prisoners as punitive and their regimes the target of bitter resentment. A small group of prisoners spent virtually all of the first two years in either A wing or D wing, with occasional periods in high control cells. Although this group of prisoners was relatively small, their presence and behaviour overshadowed virtually all other aspects of the Woodhill centres. These prisoners continually challenged, both legally and through overt disruptive behaviour, what they perceived to be the deep injustice of the system and the conditions in which they were being held. The behaviour of some prisoners became more violent and disruptive during their time in the CSC system, and as a result staff struggled to both manage the prisoners located in these regimes and to maintain a balanced approach on the other wings in an increasingly hostile and aggressive environment.

Prisoners' judgments about the legitimacy or fairness of the regimes in A and D wings were inextricably linked to their perceptions of their treatment. In turn, it was difficult in practice for staff at Woodhill to separate the notion of restricted privileges for prisoners from harsh attitudes towards them on the part of staff. The distinction between a strict regime (designed to contain and modify behaviour) and a punitive regime (designed to punish) is a fine one. Perhaps, as Alison Liebling argues, the only way to separate the concept of 'strictness' from the concept of 'punishment' is to build in a legitimate material threshold, to operate in a procedurally fair manner, and for staff to retain a neutral and decent interactive approach towards prisoners, however difficult this might be in these pressured and unsafe environments (see Appendix 1).

Progression and the IEP framework

The Spurr Report identified behavioural change and long-term containment as the necessarily dual aims of the CSC system. The system's dual function, however, was arguably underplayed, so that in the early stages, more thought went into the progressive side than into the regressive option, or the downward spiral. This emphasis on progression meant that staff were unprepared for, and unsettled by, those prisoners who actively challenged the system and refused to cooperate and 'progress'.

Despite clear signals in the Spurr Report that some prisoners would require long-term stays, staff had expected to receive prisoners who were prepared to progress. Thus there were few contingency plans for how to manage those prisoners who did not want to co-operate. It was only in the second year of operation that it was formally acknowledged that some prisoners would require long-term containment, some because of the high risk they represented on normal location, others because of their non-cooperative behaviour within the CSC system.

The IEP scheme operating within the CSC system did little in terms of encouraging prisoners to progress or cooperate with the system. IEP was seen as remarkably irrelevant to this group of prisoners by staff, and by the prisoners themselves. There were two major flaws in the application of IEP to this population: (i) the assumption of a 'rational choice' model and instrumental reasoning on the part of these prisoners; and (ii) the notion that compliance and progression could be equated with suitability for return to the mainstream of some of the particularly high-risk prisoners.

Rational choice

The IEP framework depends on a rational choice model of human behaviour; an instrumental reasoning which locates material rewards and punishments at the core of motivation. The suitability of such a model for the CSC population is questionable. At the very least such a model assumes a capacity for dispassionate decision making, which given the mental health problems of a large number of these prisoners and the degree of distrust and antagonism towards prison authorities, may perhaps have been an unduly optimistic assumption. Additionally such a model fails to take into consideration the less 'rational' factors that often motivate prisoner behaviour and the pressures that arise from the culture of prison life which influence prisoner behaviour.

Compliance and risk reduction

The IEP system is based on the prisoner receiving increasing privileges on the basis of compliant behaviour. Within the CSCs, however, both compliance and risk reduction were necessary for progression. This dual assessment of prisoners could cause confusion amongst prisoners and staff. Prisoners were unsure of what was expected of them if they complied with the regime but still did not progress. This could become a source of frustration amongst some prisoners.

Staff were in the difficult position, with some prisoners, of encouraging them to cooperate with the system knowing that they could not move beyond a certain stage due to the risk they presented. Since prisoners could only receive higher privileges if they moved on to a higher centre these prisoners who cooperated gained nothing from their cooperation. Woodhill has been trying to address this particular problem by enhancing individual prisoners' regimes within the constraints of the Restricted Regime Centre.

For some prisoners, therefore, their compliant behaviour could not be rewarded in adherence to an earned privilege scheme if their risk assessment remained unacceptably high:

> In this sense, of there being a distinction between compliant behaviour (over which it was assumed prisoners had some control) and a reduction in risk posed (which might include behaviour seen as disordered or not within the prisoner's control), the 'carrot and stick' element of IEP was an illusion.
>
> (Liebling Appendix 1:22)

A clearer indication of the role of risk in their assessments would perhaps help prisoners to be more realistic about the time they are likely to spend in the different centres. Similarly, more thorough risk assessment procedures would increase the likelihood of identifying the true risk which prisoners may represent. More detailed and comprehensive risk assessments might also allow identification of the environments most likely to sustain prisoners' behaviour, which could offer more management options for dealing with those few prisoners who present an exceptional risk both within the CSC system and on normal location.

To date the manner in which prisoners' improved behaviour, and hence suitability to progress, has been judged remains unclear and in many ways subjective. Compliance with the regime in general appeared to be the main criterion by which prisoners were judged. Compliance with the regime, however, was no guarantee that the underlying causes of their disruptive behaviour had been addressed and that the level of risk in terms of disruptive behaviour had decreased nor that their ability to function on normal location had increased.

Final destination

The degree to which the CSC system differs from that of the mainstream prison system has implications for the overall goal of the system for the majority of prisoners, viz. progressing them back to normal location. The degree to which the system prepares the prisoners for return to normal location is questionable. Without doubt the system serves an important role in providing these prisoners a space in which to stabilise themselves and address their disruptive behaviour for the first time in many years.

Within the CSC system prisoners received considerable support from staff and as a result of the small numbers would receive answers to queries and concerns relatively quickly. The environments, therefore, within the CSCs were very different to the ones they would be returned to. There was almost a paradox to the situation, the majority of the prisoners needed the increased support and supervision to address their problems but this would be the thing that would be absent once they returned to normal location.

In terms of the final transition back to normal location the gap between the final stage of the CSC system was considerable. Prisoners, in general, went straight from a small unit that was staff intensive back to a dispersal wing which would hold considerably higher numbers of prisoners and fewer staff. Merely becoming accustomed to the numbers of prisoners and the accompanying noise and bustle would be challenging for the prisoners. Managing this particular transition is essential to increasing the likelihood of prisoners remaining on normal location.

In the process of translating the policy of the Spurr Report into practice the broad notion of progression implicit in the report, and the high level of flexibility required to achieve it, became subsumed by a simple adherence to a set of 'carrot and stick' principles and practices – albeit mainly 'stick'. The notion that prisoners were likely to respond in the 'instrumental' and 'rational choice' way assumed by a CSC system founded on 'progression' was unrealistic.

9. Integration with the long-term prison system

As part of the terms of reference for our evaluation of the CSC system, we were invited to consider whether the centres were adequately integrated with the rest of the long-term prison system, both from the management's perspective and from the perspective of individual inmates and their prison careers. In addition to our general observation of how the system appeared to operate, in relation to the rest of the long-term system, we made a series of special visits to each of the five dispersal prisons at the end of the first and second years of the evaluation. We discussed with staff their experience of the CSC system, including the use of the high control cells (HCCs), visited their segregation units and talked about the process and preparation for receiving deselected CSC prisoners back onto normal location. We hoped to interview any prisoners currently held in each prison at the time of our visit but, although several expressed a willingness to be seen by us, in the event only one such interview took place, with an ex-CSC prisoner who had been settled on normal location in a dispersal prison for several weeks.

Knowledge of the CSC system

Despite a number of initiatives, e.g. presentations and 'information stalls' at national Prison Service conferences, the CSC system still appeared unfamiliar and peripheral to the long-term prison system. Awareness and knowledge of the CSC system was still quite limited, even after being in operation for over two years. Comparatively little was known in the dispersal prisons about the regimes provided or the individual treatment of disruptive prisoners at the different Centres.

Most of the knowledge of the system that existed tended to be related to the Woodhill centres, which were generally perceived in almost wholly negative terms, as 'nothing but a large segregation unit' or 'a big cage'. This could be explained not only by the wider publicity given to the dirty protests and other problems at Woodhill, but also because the main contact between the CSC system and the high security estate so far had been through the use of the high control cells for some exceptionally disruptive and difficult prisoners. In contrast, there had been very few cases of prisoners being deselected from the CSCs and successfully re-integrated into the mainstream, on normal location.

Very little appeared to be known about either I wing or the Activity Intervention Centres (G wing), at Durham except in one dispersal prison where they had referred a few prisoners to I wing. The information flow was still seen to be poor and not conducive to the development of closer working relationships between CSCs and high security prisons.

Exchanges of information between centres and the rest of the long-term prison estate appeared mainly to take the form of informal communication (a common feature found throughout the Prison Service) rather than through a more structured system of information sharing. Staff in long-term prisons, particularly those in segregation units, were keen to learn more about the system and recommended that some sort of brochure be produced which could be sent to all prisons informing them of what the CSC system did and how it operated. However, towards the latter half of the second year, at least two dispersal prisons had begun to arrange staff exchanges/visits by their segregation unit staff to Woodhill, which were seen as very valuable – even if these visits sometimes only served to confirm the negative picture dispersal staff had already formed of Woodhill, especially of A and D wings.

High control cells

Although each of the high security prisons had held prisoners in its HCCs during the past two years, the level of communication between the prisons and Woodhill concerning these prisoners was fairly minimal. This was partly due to the fact that whilst prisoners were in the HCC all that was required of the segregation staff was to 'hold them' – for up to 56 days. Officially, the regime and conditions for CSC prisoners held in high control cells should broadly reflect the standards of D wing at Woodhill. Towards the end of 1999 steps had been taken to ensure consistent standards in the HCCs and guidelines had been issued stipulating what the HCCs should provide.

Nevertheless, in practice there was a certain degree of flexibility, with prisoners being normally managed in accordance with the local segregation unit guidelines. It was exceptional, for example, for segregation unit staff to continue to unlock prisoners in full C&R kit. After an initial assessment period, the prisoner would be managed in a similar manner to most segregation prisoners although the staffing levels would tend to remain higher (though not in all cases) and the prisoner would be unlocked by himself at all times.

In one dispersal prison, a consolidated regime document had been produced for the management of prisoners in the high control cell. Once moved to a HCC, CSC prisoners generally behaved well and 'kept their heads down'. Segregation staff felt that prisoners used their time in HCCs to take a break from the CSCs and to recover their energy to continue 'their fight' with the CSC system on their return. Prior to the return of the prisoner to the CSC, a member of the dispersal segregation unit was required to debrief the CSC unit manager about the prisoner's behaviour and attitude.

Return of CSC prisoners to the mainstream

Since very few prisoners were returned to mainstream prisons in the first two years of the CSC system's operation, no specific re-entry policies had been put in place by the CSCs and little attention had been given in most of the dispersals to appropriate procedures or plans for reintegrating deselected CSC prisoners back onto normal location. From our discussions with dispersal staff, it seemed likely that in the majority of cases a returning CSC prisoner would be placed either in the segregation unit or on a basic wing for an initial period of induction/assessment. This was in line with the standard practice when receiving prisoners who had the potential to be troublesome or were an unknown quantity.

However, in May 2000, draft procedures were in the process of being drawn up for transferring Durham CSC prisoners to normal location in the mainstream. These new procedures involve the provision of a *transition plan*, which identifies a suitable establishment for the prisoner; both the prisoner and the receiving establishment must have given their provisional agreement to the transfer. Once the transfer has been agreed in principle, a detailed two-way process of information sharing and communication about the prisoner's background and needs will then be put in place between Durham CSC staff and staff of the receiving establishment. This will involve visits by the prisoner's CSC personal officer to the receiving prison prior to the transfer and at least once within six weeks of the transfer. In fact, in the cases of the two prisoners returned to mainstream prison to date, G wing staff ensured considerable involvement from the receiving prison's staff, and it is this sort of good practice on which the new procedures seek to build and develop.

The transfer process is obviously a vital and sensitive one for all parties concerned, and needs to be handled with the utmost care to ensure the successful reintegration of the prisoner. A degree of trust in the judgement and assessments of staff in the other establishment will be required, which may not always come easily in a service where there appears to be a degree of scepticism and distrust regarding the judgement of staff and specialists in other prisons about how a particular prisoner might behave and ought to be managed when transferred to a different establishment, with its own traditions, history and inmate culture.

A shared professionalism must be fostered in order to help the prisoner cope with what will inevitably be a huge 'culture shock' when returning to normal location in the mainstream after several years 'out of circulation' in the CSCs – and before that on CAS, or in long-term segregation. The suggestion in the draft procedures that consideration should be given to a short supervised period on normal location in Durham prison prior to transition seems an eminently sensible way to try to ease the transition.

In view of the understandable anxiety and doubts voiced by many CSC prisoners about the likelihood of their being offered a fair opportunity on return to normal location, it is vital for them to be fully involved in the process of preparation for their transfer. In particular, it is important to make it clear to them that they might have to spend an initial period of time in restricted conditions for purposes of assessment. Otherwise moving from the relative openness of the Activity Intervention Centre to restricted conditions may be interpreted as a sign that staff were not willing to give them a chance and the prisoner may well react adversely and all the hard work that had gone before could be undone by lack of communication.

Prospects for closer working

There is still considerable scope for improving the level of integration between the CSC system and the long-term prison estate. In some respects the low level of integration is not surprising as there have been so few referrals to the system and so few prisoners returned to mainstream prisons. Exchanges of staff are planned between segregation staff in two of the dispersal prisons visited and Woodhill staff (from A and D wing) and it is likely that this will further promote the CSC system in the long-term estate. It should also be of benefit to the Woodhill staff who, although managing the prisoners well, have had limited experience of working with long-term prisoners in segregation conditions. These exchanges offer the possibility of the sharing of good practices between the prisons.

In terms of the information available about the CSC system, it mainly related (and not always accurately) to conditions and events in A and D wings. Much less was known about the more positive end of the CSC system in Woodhill and Durham, which could have implications for the kind of referrals prisons might consider making. Ways of publicising the more constructive aspects of the CSC system should be explored and developed.

Particularly in view of the virtual stalemate that existed on D wing throughout the second year, consideration might be given to using the time prisoners spend in HCCs more constructively. Since the majority of prisoners have been more amenable to staff whilst in

HCCs (although this was also considered to be part of the prisoners 'campaign' against the system), ways could be explored of using dispersal segregation staff in some sort of intermediary role. As communication between staff and prisoners is virtually non-existent on D wing, and in the cases of some prisoners their anger and aggressive behaviour has been increasing during the time they have spent in the CSC system, working with the prisoners while they are in HCCs might offer an avenue for discharging some of that anger (in a way that doesn't involve violence) and would also provide support for staff working on D wing as they would no longer be the only ones managing these prisoners.

Once removed from the antagonistic 'no-win' environment that D wing has become, prisoners might be better able to express and perhaps come to terms with their resentment of the system, so that solutions to their present predicament might be more likely to emerge. Using the high control cells in a more proactive manner would also help increase the level of integration between the CSC system and the high security prison estate, with each having a higher investment in the other and developing a sense of 'shared ownership' of the problems and successes achieved.

10. Objectives and achievements of the CSC system

The five official aims and functions of the Close Supervision Centres, as set down in the revised Operating Standards (April 1999), may be summarised as follows:

(i)   removal of the most seriously disruptive prisoners from mainstream prisons;

ii)   safe containment of those prisoners in small highly supervised units;

(iii)   provision of opportunities to address anti-social disruptive behaviour;

(iv)   to stabilise prisoner behaviour and prepare them for a safe return to the mainstream;

(v)   long-term containment of those who continue to pose a serious threat to the safety of staff and prisoners.

We first summarise the main findings of our evaluation, and then consider how far each of the above aims of the CSCs appears to have been achieved to date. The final section of this Report considers the implications of our findings for the future development of the CSC system.

I   Summary of main findings

Prisoner selection

In its first two years of operation, the CSC system managed a total of 51 prisoners. Over half of these prisoners had previously spent time on the Continuous Assessment Scheme (CAS), which was formally closed in February 1999.

Seventeen of the 38 prisoners on the CAS scheme in February 1998 (when the CSC system was first established) were not transferred to CSCs but managed in some other way. However, apart from one prisoner who subsequently assaulted an officer, virtually all those ex-CAS prisoners appeared to have settled down on normal location within dispersal or other long-term prisons.

Forty-six prisoners were referred to the CSC Selection Committee in the first two years, on one or more occasions, of whom 22 were selected for the CSCs. A follow-up of those prisoners who were turned down for the CSCs showed that three-quarters of them continued to be held within the dispersal system without causing any further serious trouble.

It can be concluded, therefore, that the CSC selection process was generally quite successful in identifying those prisoners who were formerly on CAS or newly referred to the Committee but who could be safely managed without having recourse to the CSC system.

Available recorded information about the previous criminal and penal histories of the prisoners who were managed by the CSCs over this period confirmed that all but perhaps one prisoner fitted one or more of the official CSC selection criteria, having extensive records of serious violence and disruptive behaviour both inside and outside prison. The selection process for one other prisoner was perhaps rather questionable.

Population trends

The number of prisoners held in the Woodhill CSCs at the end of the first year was 24. In the second year, a total of 36 prisoners were managed at Woodhill, with the average population being 26. Of these, 11 prisoners spent their time being moved between A wing and D wing – with seven of them also being moved out to high control cells for periods totalling 4–6 months each. Eight prisoners refused to cooperate with the system throughout most of the first two years.

Sixteen prisoners in Woodhill could be said to have been attempting more or less consistently to work with the system in order to progress, spending their time on B and C wings. During the second year, eight prisoners progressed from the Woodhill CSCs to the Activity Intervention Centre in Durham G wing; a further three prisoners progressed from Woodhill to Durham I wing.

Durham I wing managed an average of eight prisoners for most of its first two years, with its lowest number in the second year being six. Four prisoners spent the whole of the second year located on I wing.

Durham G wing opened in May 1999. It continued to hold a non-CSC high-risk prisoner for its first 3–4 months, with the build up of its CSC prisoner numbers being quite slow – reaching seven by the end of its first year (April 2000). Two prisoners had been progressed from G wing to normal location in the mainstream, with several other prisoners likely to be deselected in the near future. Two prisoners were returned to Woodhill for renewed disruptive behaviour.

Three of the prisoners in G wing are likely to need long-term containment in the CSC system, due to the high risk they continue to pose to the safety of staff and/or prisoners, and despite having complied with the system sufficiently to progress to G wing.

Regime provision in the CSCs
Woodhill – C wing
In the first year virtually no constructive activities had been provided for prisoners on the Programmes Intervention Centre (C wing) at Woodhill. Part of this situation may have been due to the small number of prisoners held in C wing in that first year, and the generally very short time that CSC prisoners remained on the wing before being progressed to the Activity Intervention Centre in Hull A wing.

The situation on the wing showed some slight improvement in the second year, but there was still a high level of boredom and inactivity (for both prisoners and staff) on C wing throughout most of the period. Some of the professional and resource problems surrounding the provision of appropriate group work on C wing were eventually resolved, so that two Enhanced Thinking Skills (ETS) courses were provided in 1999.

Woodhill – B wing
The central role of the Structured Regime Centre (B wing) at Woodhill in the CSC system was that of providing an assessment of the prisoners at the point of entry to the system, that should then inform the choices and decisions that have to be made about their initial location and future progress. Although a version of the Dispersal Induction Assessment (DIA) was piloted on B wing, wider questions need to be raised not only about the feasibility of implementing a suitable assessment tool, including the role of specialists in that process (see below), but also about the most appropriate time and place for assessing CSC prisoners.

The main problem on B wing throughout the second year continued to be the struggle that staff faced simply in carrying out the basic daily routines of unlocking, feeding, showering and exercising prisoners. Given the chronic staff shortages, the time and energy that these routine handling tasks consumed meant that there was little time or energy left for more constructive activities and meaningful staff-prisoner interaction.

Woodhill – A wing

Prisoners' perceptions of the regime on the Restricted Regime Centre (A wing) were very negative throughout the two year period. There were very few signs of the wing being able to fulfil its intended role in the CSC progressive system, in which staff were supposed to encourage prisoners to move up to B wing. Although the Operating Standards were revised to ensure that the physical conditions in A wing were comparable with those in dispersal segregation units, this had little effect on prisoners' perception of the almost wholly punitive impact of the Restricted Regime Centre.

Woodhill – D wing

D wing did not fulfil its original role as the segregation unit for the CSC wings, but had to cope with persistently confrontational behaviour from a group of prisoners who refused to cooperate with the CSC system and were engaged in acts of concerted indiscipline, dirty protests and violence/threats of violence against staff. Whilst fully appreciating the real dangers to which staff were exposed on a daily basis in D wing, it would be difficult to claim that the resultant conditions and regime on D wing were either humane or acceptable.

Durham – I wing

The role of Durham I wing within the CSC system was to provide a therapeutic regime with psychological and psychiatric support, particularly for those prisoners whose disruptive behaviour was linked to their psychiatric and mental health. There was a target of 20 hours constructive activity per week.

One of the main characteristics of I wing throughout the first two years was the high level of staff-prisoner interaction. There was, however, a significant reduction in the psychological input to the centre in the second year, following the resignation of the experienced senior psychologist in June 1999. No full-time replacement was found until the end of the year and this had a considerable effect on the amount of specialist individual and group work that was done with prisoners.

Durham – G wing

Durham G wing was handicapped, in its early days, by the lack of adequate preparation for the transfer of the Activity Intervention Centre from Hull A wing, which closed earlier than anticipated. As a result, and due to the general shortage of psychological and psychiatric resources at Durham, it was unable to provide the individual counselling and programmes that it would have wished. Although a part-time clinical psychologist was later appointed and undertook some individual work with two prisoners in G wing, there was a failure to deliver the regime stipulated in Operational Standards.

Management and staffing issues
Staff turnover and retention
All the CSCs experienced considerable changes in their management structures and senior managers during the first two years. In addition, particularly at Woodhill, there was a significant turnover of uniformed staff which, combined with the overall staff shortage, increased the pressures on existing staff to carry out their essential duties. Furthermore, it was often difficult to recruit enough suitable volunteers to work in the Woodhill CSCs in view of the well-publicised problems being experienced in the handling of the prisoners on A and D wings.

There were fewer problems of staff retention and recruitment at Durham, largely because of the more positive profile that work in the CSCs continued to enjoy there. However, several staff were coming to the end of their initial 'tour of duty' on I wing, where the nature of the staff-prisoner interaction made it vital to retain as much continuity as possible and to recruit officers with a strong commitment to the ethos of the wing.

Staff morale and effectiveness
There were also a number of broader issues relating to the local management of the centres at Durham and Woodhill that affected staff morale and effectiveness. For example, the different centres at Woodhill did not enjoy the same degree of operational autonomy that was apparent at Durham and which contributed significantly to the development of the positive staff culture and 'camaraderie' that was so distinctive of I and G wings.

At Woodhill, in contrast, particularly in the early months, the events on A and D wings (concerted indiscipline, dirty protests etc) clearly affected all the CSC staff to some degree, including those working in B and C wings, and achieved just the sort of pervasive and undermining impact upon the new system that many of the 'protesting' prisoners wanted. Although this was an exceptional and, to some extent, largely unanticipated set of circumstances it nevertheless highlighted the problems inherent in the physical design and staffing arrangements of the Woodhill CSCs.

One of the results was the eventual emergence of a fairly clear split within the Woodhill CSCs at the beginning of the second year between A and D wings, on the one hand, focusing on control and containment and B and C wings, on the other, working towards progressing the prisoners through the CSC system. This 'de facto' division of aims and ethos within Woodhill seemed unlikely to help towards the development of an integrated system based on the original progressive aims of the CSCs.

Local autonomy issues

Because of the high political and media profile of the CSCs, it was understandable that they should receive a great deal of attention from senior Prison Service management. The result was that many management decisions about CSC matters, that arguably should have been handled by various levels of local management, were 'pushed up' to a higher level. This deprived senior, middle and lower managers in the CSCs of the opportunities and responsibilities for making their own decisions. The net effect was an undermining of the confidence of staff at different levels in their ability to do the jobs that their rank would normally entail.

The role of psychiatry and psychology
The incidence of mental illness

The psychiatric assessment of the CSC prisoners revealed the extent and seriousness of mental disorder among this population, in particular their high rates of mental illness and its co-occurrence with personality disorder. The implications of these findings are serious in relation to the provision of clinical services and in relation to those prisoners who have been kept in solitary confinement in D wing for extended periods.

Inadequate assessment systems

The emergent picture of prevalent mental disorder amongst the CSC prisoners was particularly disturbing in view of the lack of adequate psychiatric support for the CSC system from the outset and the relatively limited input that forensic psychiatrists and psychologists have had in the assessment process on B wing. These assessments have been seriously handicapped by the refusal of many prisoners to have anything to do with the psychologists; and most provide little psychological or historical understanding of the prisoners' personalities and emotional lives.

There was a lack of relevant knowledge about the personalities, background and motivation of the CSC prisoners at virtually every stage in the system, starting at the point of referral and selection, through that of initial assessment and continuing into the centres themselves where individual and group work with prisoners was intended to address their disruptive behaviour and enable them to progress through the system. Prisoner records and professional relationships with prisoners should if possible be of a kind that enable sound psychological knowledge of the prisoners to be established. This does not carry connotations of being 'soft', collusive or losing objectivity. Well based psychological understanding facilitates safety and security because it usefully informs judgements about prisoners' responses, and predictions of risk.

The effects of the CSCs on prisoners' behaviour

Despite the development of a containment role for the CSCs, the notion of 'progression' has remained central to the system. Therefore, the number of prisoners who progress through the system and are returned to normal location remains one of the key bench-marks for measuring the 'success' of the CSC system as a whole. On this criterion, the system cannot be said to have enjoyed a great deal of success in its first two years.

Between February 1998 and May 2000, 12 prisoners were transferred out of CSCs, either to special hospitals (four) or normal location in the mainstream. Two of the prisoners transferred to special hospitals were subsequently returned to the prison system (because of renewed violence) and re-referred to the CSCs. Of the prisoners returned to normal location, only four have so far been able to settle without any recurrence of their disruptive behaviour. In summary, therefore, two-thirds of the prisoners who progressed from the CSC system in its first 28 months failed to survive their departure from the centres.

Another way of assessing the impact of the CSCs on prisoners' behaviour – at least in the short-term – is to compare their disruptiveness whilst in the centres with their pattern of behaviour prior to their admission to the CSCs. On the basis of the data available to us, and taking account of their locations prior to CSC selection, we concluded that 30 prisoners showed a reduced level of disruptive behaviour in the CSCs, compared with their record outside the system, whereas six prisoners showed an increased level of assaultive behaviour in the CSCs. The remaining ten prisoners, for whom we had information, showed little change in either direction.

A group of eight prisoners refused to cooperate with the system from the outset and embarked upon a persistent campaign of confrontation and challenge, involving dirty protests, violence and/or threats of violence against staff, as well as litigation against the system. In the cases of some of these prisoners, their behaviour deteriorated dramatically following their transfer to the CSC, and it would be unwise to claim that the overall effect of the CSCs on these prisoners had been anything other than very negative.

The impact of the CSC system on the dispersal estate

There is no comprehensive data set for measuring accurately the levels of disruptive behaviour in the dispersal estate before and after February 1998; nor, if such data were available, is there any way of attributing any changes with any degree of certainty solely to the influence of the CSCs. So many other management initiatives and changes have been introduced into the long-term prison system during the past five years, that any or all of these could have contributed to the improved situation in dispersals. Nevertheless, there are a number of indicators that suggest to us that the CSCs may possibly have made a contribution to reducing the level of disruptive behaviour and facilitating the management of order in dispersals.

Data from the Prison Service's incident recording system and 'Order and Control' matrix, for the three years preceding and the two years following the introduction of the CSCs, confirmed that there had been an overall reduction in serious incidents in dispersal prisons in 1998 and 1999. Reductions were apparent in hostage taking, concerted acts of indiscipline and assaults on prisoners and staff. A note of caution about the interpretation of these statistics must be made, as there are also indications of a general reduction of serious incidents and assaults in the prison system as a whole, which could not be claimed to be directly influenced by the existence of the CSCs.

Discussions with staff at dispersal prisons over the past two years, and visits to their segregation units, confirmed the view that not only had the CSC system taken out of circulation a group of very disruptive prisoners that made their work less stressful and dangerous, but provided relief from the task of coping with the 'merry-go-round' of CAS prisoners. The few prisoners held in the CSC high control cells, now available in each dispersal, were far less intrusive than was the CAS system.

The number of prisoners being held in dispersal segregation units on a long-term basis has significantly decreased in the past two or three years, which has allowed them to develop a range of promising initiatives for the handling of any difficult behaviour on the part of their own prisoners – thereby hopefully preventing them from becoming future candidates for referral to the CSCs.

Cost effectiveness

The critical factor in the consideration of the cost effectiveness of the CSC system is the assessment of the benefits it has generated. Unfortunately, in designing the system apparently little consideration was given to the nature of the potential benefits or how they might be realised. Consequently, there is no solid foundation on which to base an evaluation. Further complexity has been added to this situation, as the anticipated outcomes of the system proved elusive and operational objectives were changed.

Although the fieldwork revealed several aspects of the management of disruptive prisoners which have been improved, either directly or indirectly as a consequence of the CSCs, many of the findings are subjective and some more speculative. To attempt to place a value on such effects would require an even greater degree of speculation and a high risk of misrepresentation.

In some respects the value of the contribution of the CSC system is relatively hard to establish in the context of an impact study such as this. The benefits of the system may become more apparent when the effect on the pattern of prisoner behaviour can be assessed from a longer term perspective. However, given the severe limitations of the data and the difficulty in isolating the effects of the CSCs from other changes, it is unlikely that a formal benefit evaluation of this episode will be feasible.

Although the CSC units are not identifiable cost centres in Prison Service accounting data, by focusing the management of disruptive prisoners in a small number of centres the costs are more readily identifiable. Our central estimate of the cost per annum of a place in the CSC system implies that the incremental cost against the benchmark of normal accommodation in a dispersal prison is of the order of £55k. However, the full economic cost may have been substantially greater, though this is partly accounted for by the transitional conditions under which the system has operated throughout the period.

Although retrospective analysis at some future date might clarify the benefits of the CSCs and enable a formal evaluation of at least some aspects of their effect, our tentative conclusion is that they are unlikely to be judged cost effective in purely accounting terms. If cost effectiveness is to be used in assessing the future development in the management of highly disruptive prisoners or other groups where special provision is required, more consideration must be given to the identification, monitoring and systematic recording of outcomes and effect.

In the light of our findings, we shall now briefly revisit the five official aims and functions of the CSC system to examine the extent to which these appear to have been achieved to date.

II   The aims of the CSC system and their achievement

1.   The removal of seriously disruptive prisoners from mainstream prisons

The 51 prisoners managed by the CSC system in its first two years were clearly prisoners who had caused serious disruption in dispersals; over half of them had been in the CAS system immediately prior to transfer to the CSCs and many of the rest were being held in dispersal segregation units.

The CSC selection process appears to have been quite successful in identifying those who posed a continuing threat of disruption, as the vast majority of those not selected subsequently appear to have settled down in normal location.

Following the establishment of the CSC system in 1998, and a reduction in the number being held long-term in dispersal segregation units, dispersal prisons have been in a better position to manage successfully any disruptive behaviour that may occur, thereby hopefully preventing the emergence of a new generation of persistently disruptive prisoners.

2. The safe containment of prisoners in the CSCs

There appears to have been a reduction in the disruptive behaviour of a majority of CSC prisoners following transfer into the system; however, violence and serious threats to the safety of staff came from a significant minority of prisoners in Woodhill who refused to cooperate with the system and adopted a persistently confrontational stance.

Furthermore, the behaviour of this group of prisoners (located in A and D wings) affected staff working in B and C wings, who were not able to feel safe from actual or threatened violence. Pressure was put on B wing prisoners by those in A wing not to cooperate, and several incidents of fighting occurred between prisoners in C wing.

Similarly, in the more open conditions of Durham I and G wings (and before that in Hull A wing), prisoners expressed real concerns about their safety, being in such close proximity to some notorious and manifestly unpredictable prisoners.

Even D wing, with its very controlled and stark environment, was not perceived by staff or prisoners as a safe environment, but as one that posed real threats to the personal safety of staff and prisoners, as well as to the mental health of those held in solitary confinement there for any length of time.

3. The provision of opportunities to address disruptive behaviour

The structured regimes of Durham I and G wings allowed positive interaction to take place between staff and prisoners, who generally welcomed the opportunities presented to address their disruptive behaviour and recognise the benefit of cooperating with the system in this way. Although Durham experienced problems relating to specialist psychological and psychiatric support in the second year, a staff-prisoner 'community culture' continued to flourish (especially in I wing) which was very conducive to bringing about change in prisoners.

In contrast, B and C wings at Woodhill have so far largely failed to achieve this objective, partly because of the lack of an effective assessment system to indicate the individual and group work that needed to be done with these prisoners, and partly because of a failure to recognise (in many cases) that tackling their mental health needs was an essential prerequisite to helping them address their anti-social behaviour.

4. To stabilise prisoners' behaviour and prepare them for a safe return to the mainstream

There is evidence that the behaviour of perhaps one third of CSC prisoners may have been 'stabilised' to some extent during their time in the centres – although this was obviously not the case with the group of prisoners who refused to cooperate with the system nor for many of those who failed to progress satisfactorily through the system.

In the first two years, 12 prisoners (less than a quarter of the total) progressed through the CSC system and were transferred out, either to special hospitals (four) or to normal location in the mainstream prison system. Of these, two prisoners were subsequently returned to prison from the Special Hospitals and reselected for the CSCs, with only four prisoners appearing to have settled on normal location. Despite it being 'early days' yet for the CSC system, the number of cases of successful reintegration and return to the mainstream seems low, in the context of the official overall objective of progression.

There were a few cases where the CSC system identified mentally ill prisoners and managed to transfer them to special hospitals, but there were often serious delays and problems in the working relations between the CSCs and the mental health services, indicating that this area needs further close attention if it is to work in the best interests of such prisoners. The two examples of men returned to the prison system from special hospitals raise the question of whether the high-security hospitals are currently able to manage the most dangerous mentally disordered prisoners. If they lack equivalent capacity to the prison system to manage violence, this may mean that a group of the most dangerous mentally disordered offenders are effectively excluded from psychiatric hospital care.

5. Long-term containment of high-risk prisoners

This fifth function for the CSCs was added to the Operating Standards in April 1999, because of the emergence of two particular groups of prisoners, namely (i) those whose aggressive non-compliance undermined the central notion of progression, and (ii) those whose assessed risk was too great for them to be returned to the mainstream – despite having met the other criteria for 'progression'. The CSC system is currently failing to deal adequately with either of these two groups of prisoners.

The regimes obtaining in Woodhill A and D wings are not appropriate for the long-term control and containment role which they have been required to fulfil in the last two years, as evidenced by the group of non-cooperating prisoners who have been shuttled to and fro between A and D wings, plus occasional 56 day 'cooling off' periods in a high control cell in the dispersal estate.

Similarly, alternative provision is necessary for the small number of prisoners who may meet the criteria for progression through the system to Durham G or I wings, but are too dangerous and of unpredictably high risk to be returned to normal location either for a very long time or perhaps for ever. To keep them indefinitely on G wing would not only be potentially dangerous for other prisoners and staff but would affect the dynamics of a wing that is intended as a re-entry unit for preparing prisoners to return to the mainstream.

11.   Key issues for the future development of the CSC system

We conclude by highlighting some of the key issues that need to be addressed in developing an effective and humane strategy for the management of disruptive prisoners. Any new developments should be firmly grounded in the increasing body of knowledge relating to the personalities and mental health of these prisoners, and the strategies they adopt for coping with the stresses of imprisonment. We draw primarily on the findings that have emerged from our evaluation over the past two years, but also borrow ideas and insights that may already be under consideration by the Prison Service for the future development of the CSC system.

Underlying assumptions and principles

We believe that the central underlying principle of prisoner 'progression', through a variety of incentives and earned privileges, is seriously flawed with respect to the management of these prisoners – particularly if there is an unreasonably austere and restrictive starting point.

The events of the last two and a half years have shown that the behaviour of the prisoners admitted to the CSC system is far more complex than was generally recognised at the outset. The 'privileges' on offer were not perceived by many prisoners as of relevance or value to their individual situations. As a result many failed to respond to the incentives for progression but instead challenged the system's basic principles and the fairness of its procedures and practices.

At the root of the problem, in our view, is a lack of proper understanding and appreciation of the background histories and damaging experiences which these prisoners bring with them into the CSC system. These personal histories and experiences have frequently been associated with the prison system and in many cases are linked to and/or have contributed to disturbed mental states. Accordingly, the progressive principle is unrealistic.

The management of disruptive prisoners should, therefore, be based on a set of rather different operational principles and processes. The key elements should include (i) a comprehensive assessment process; (ii) the establishment of differential regimes, with safe and humane conditions; and (iii) the long-term containment of high-risk prisoners.

Assessment and case management

Because disruptive prisoners are a very heterogeneous group, each with their own individual histories, emotions and attitudes, a comprehensive assessment is a vital first stage in their proper management. Ideally, such an assessment should be prepared at a much earlier stage in their prison sentence (as is intended for the DIA), but certainly at or before the point of referral to the CSC Selection Committee. This assessment must include substantial and integrated clinical input from forensic psychiatric services and others, in order to identify personality disorder and mental illness, and to assess risk.

To assist this process, ways must be found of encouraging and enabling CSC prisoners to engage with the psychologists and other specialists, who are in a position to help them address the underlying causes of their behaviour. Greater efforts should be made to 'listen' to (without necessarily condoning) the prisoners' accounts of their penal experiences and explanations of their behaviour, and to be more responsive to their interpretations and perceived needs, in order to help them find a 'way back in'.

The psychological assessment (incorporating appropriate risk assessment instruments) would provide the basis for the subsequent management of the prisoner within (or outside) the CSC system. To achieve this, there needs to be an urgent review of the psychological and psychiatric resources available to the CSC system, to enable them to implement the individual management programme for each prisoner. Successful implementation will require close working relationships with basic grade and supervisory staff in each centre (for whom there are obvious training implications), as well as with education and probation staff, and liaison with the special hospitals and outside agencies, where appropriate.

Differential regimes

Because of the progressive system's serious limitations when applied to these kinds of prisoners, a more appropriate set of operating principles and practices needs to be established. The minimum threshold should be standards and conditions that equate to or are better than those found in dispersal segregation units. These should obtain in the induction/assessment wing, where prisoners would normally expect to stay for a relatively short time until decisions have been taken about their future management.

The other wings at Woodhill and Durham should then provide a non-hierarchical range of regimes, matched to the control requirements and development needs of individual prisoners, and to be used with maximum flexibility. The standards and conditions on these other wings should be comparable to those found on normal location in dispersal prisons. Deselection could be possible from any centre, although consideration might be given to establishing a small dedicated unit for preparing prisoners for return to the mainstream.

Prisoners whose behaviour or attitudes on reception suggest that they are unlikely to cooperate with the system should be held initially (but for only a short period) in the segregation unit at Woodhill. If subsequent attempts fail to persuade them to want to work with the system, they should be returned to the dispersal system – possibly to a high control cell, depending on the nature of their disruptive or 'non-compliant' behaviour, their state of mind etc. Alternatively, there may be a case for the establishment of a dedicated unit for these prisoners, outside the CSC system, until such time as they feel able to 'sign-up' to the new aims and objectives of the CSCs.

Careful thought needs to be given to the management and staffing of the Centres in Durham and Woodhill. Wherever possible, each Centre should have its own staff complement to provide the continuity and mixture of experience/skills conducive to good staff-prisoner relationships and regime delivery. Each should be encouraged to develop its own sense of identity and distinctive role within an integrated system There should be a degree of autonomy and accountability within clearly defined parameters, so that each level of staff is engaged in tasks appropriate for that level.

Further thought should be given to the overall management structures and responsibilities for the centres at Woodhill and Durham, and also at Prison Service Headquarters. In line with the non-hierarchical principle being recommended, decisions about prisoner transfer, resource allocation and so on should be taken as openly and fairly as possible, on the basis of full consultation with all interested parties.

There is a strong case for the appointment of a full-time Director of CSCs, accountable to the Director of High Security Prisons. This would recognise the importance and demanding nature of the management of this group of prisoners, and relieve the High Security Director of some of the more routine operational decisions relating to CSCs.

Long-term containment of high-risk prisoners

There will always be a small number of disruptive prisoners whom it would be unsafe to return to normal location, even when they have spent many years in the CSC system. In a system based on the principle of progression, these prisoners have shown that they can progress through the system by satisfying the normal criteria. However, they then find themselves at the top level – but 'with nowhere to go'.

The problem has been recognised by the Prison Service, and proposals are under discussion about the nature and location of a special long-term containment unit for this group of prisoners. Removing the progressive rationale for the CSC system may help to resolve some of the problems, as it would allow more flexible movement of prisoners between centres.

Similarly, the abolition of the present framework of incentives and privileges for CSC prisoners would open up the discussion about the appropriate living conditions for these long-term containment cases, rather than being restricted by the current level of privileges available in I and G wings. Depending on logistics and resources involved, consideration should be given to providing for the special long-term containment of these prisoners in the dispersal system, outside the CSCs.

Future prospects for the prevention of disruptive behaviour

We were impressed during our visits to dispersal prisons by the innovative work being done in many segregation units to manage disruptive prisoners who might otherwise be candidates for the CSC system. It seems vital that dispersal prisons should be encouraged and properly resourced to develop this kind of 'preventive' work. In fact, the same principles of multi-disciplinary assessment and working partnerships should be applied in dispersals, and throughout the long-term prison system, as we recommend for the CSC system.

Steps should be taken to improve communications between the CSCs and the dispersal system. This will not only help them in being better prepared to receive prisoners back from the CSC system but also help them to develop a sense of shared ownership and responsibility for the behaviour of prisoners in the system as a whole. Indeed, by developing such skills in dispersal prisons the need for the CSC system will gradually diminish.

Finally, resources need to be made available for the systematic collection, monitoring and analysis of all information and data flows related to the management of disruptive prisoners. This should be used both for management purposes and for ongoing research into the nature and causes of severely disruptive behaviour. In this way it will be possible to build up a long-term knowledge base concerning difficult prisoners and their appropriate management.

References

American Psychiatric Association (1994) *Diagnostic and Statistical Manual of Mental Disorders* (4th edn). Washington: American Psychiatric Association.

Blackburn, R and Coid, JW (1999) 'Empirical clusters of DSM-III personality disorders in violent offenders'. *Journal of Personality Disorders* 13 :18–34.

Bottomley, K, Jepson, N, Elliott, K and Coid, J (1994) *Managing Difficult Prisoners: the Lincoln and Hull Special Units*. London: Home Office.

Coid, J (1991) 'Psychiatric profiles of difficult/disruptive prisoners' in K. Bottomley and W. Hay (eds) *Special Units for Difficult Prisoners*. Hull: University of Hull.

First, M B, Gibbon, M, Spitzer, R L, Williams, J B W, Benjamin, L S (1997) *Structured Clinical Interview for DSM-IV Axis II Personality Disorders (SCID-II)*. Washington DC: American Psychiatric Press Inc.

HM Inspectorate of Prisons (2000) *Inspection of Close Supervision Centres August-September 1999*. London: Home Office.

HM Prison Service/NHS Executive (1999) *The Future Organisation of Prison Health Care*. London: Home Office.

Home Office/Department of Health (1999) *Managing Dangerous People With Severe Personality Disorder: Proposals for Policy Development*. London: Home Office.

Prison Service (1996) *Management of Disruptive Prisoners: CRC Review Project Final Report* (The Spurr Report). Unpublished Report.

Singleton, N, Meltzer, H, Gatwood, R, Coid, J and Deasy, D (1998) *Psychiatric Morbidity among Prisoners in England and Wales*. London: The Stationery Office.

Spitzer, R L and Endicott, J (1979) *Schedule for Affective Disorders and Schizophrenia – Lifetime Version (SADS-L)*. New York: New York State Psychiatric Institute.

Stalenheim, E G and von-Knorring, L (1996) 'Psychopathy and Axis I and Axis II psychiatric disorders in a forensic psychiatric population in Sweden'. *Acta Psychiatrica Scandinavica* 94 217–223.

Appendix 1

Policy and practice in the management of disruptive prisoners: incentives and earned privileges, the Spurr Report and Close Supervision Centres[1]

Alison Liebling
Institute of Criminology, Cambridge

Contents

1. I would like to thank the Close Supervision Centres evaluation team (Keith Bottomley and Emma Clare, Adrian Grounds, Chris Hammond, Celia Taylor and External Assessor, Richard Sparks) for inviting me to participate in their research, for being stimulating colleagues and for their comments on this paper. My role as a consultant to the project was to explore the role of Incentives and Earned Privileges in the centres and (later) to consider the process of implementation of the Spurr Report. I would like to thank Helen Arnold for efficient and valuable research assistance during the later stages of the project and Tony Bottoms for his helpful criticism. I would also like to thank John Golds, Mike Spurr, Mike Webster, Phil Wheatley, Colette Kershaw, and Robin Carter; and staff and prisoners at Woodhill for invaluable assistance.

Summary

This paper considers the background to and implementation of the revised small units system of strict regime close supervision centres for difficult prisoners. It explores in particular some major departures from the spirit and letter of the Spurr Report which created the new centres, and the role of Incentives and Earned Privileges in their early operation. Whilst the CSC system was designed to overcome the limitations of its predecessor CRC units, and to make the management of non-consenting difficult prisoners more visible, considerable problems were experienced throughout the first two years of its operation. An exclusively utilitarian (rather than moral) motivation to comply was assumed and the material threshold of life in the revised units was austere. The dual containment and progressive function of the CSC system was insufficiently communicated to staff. Prisoners (and to some extent, staff) found it difficult to disentangle low levels of material provision from punishment. Progression was not always possible, despite relatively compliant behaviour, due to extremely high levels of risk. The broad notion of progression implicit in the Spurr Report, and the high level of flexibility required to achieve it, became subsumed by a simplistic adherence to a 'carrot and stick', but mainly stick, set of practices. The early experiences of the CSC system have much to teach about the policy-making and implementation process, as well as the handling (and mishandling) of difficult prisoners.

> He is meeting his targets. He doesn't like to be seen as compliant. He was praised by staff recently and got very upset – he saw his solicitor about it. (Senior manager)

> This lot have dug their heels in, they have settled down; they're not progressing anywhere. (Officer, Basic Regime)

> He should be lifted and brought to Woodhill, A wing [Basic Regime], so he can be given an opportunity to progress. (Senior manager)

> For me, I have come so far now, it would be insane to throw it away. After everything I've been through, I have to carry on now. This is really all psychological hate games; it's all about power and control. All the inmates want is to have their own identity. (prisoner)

1.

Introduction

In July 1995 the Prison Service Executive Committee established a project reviewing the management of a small group of prisoners presenting serious control problems, for whom the existing procedures were not effective. Their brief included a study of the feasibility of introducing a Strict Regime CRC unit. The aims of the project were:

- To ensure that appropriate options were available to deal with disruptive prisoners in order to relieve pressure on the mainstream;

- To provide a means to encourage disruptive prisoners to cease being disruptive.

The context in which the review took place was the period of two high profile sets of escapes from Whitemoor and Parkhurst dispersal prisons in 1994 and 1995 respectively (Home Office 1994; 1995). The escapes (which resulted in the sacking of the then Director General of the Prison Service, Derek Lewis, and the departure of two Governors and an Area Manager) were linked in official reports to an underenforcement by staff of security and other procedures in the interests of 'good order' and easy going relationships with prisoners. This analysis – and perhaps especially the reconsideration of security as a social-dynamic process incorporating control – led to the deliberate reshaping of the dispersal estate to regain some of the power base staff had lost – or barely achieved in two of the newly opening dispersal prisons – and to communicate to prisoners that the prison service was in charge of its regimes for long term prisoners. This was (successfully) accomplished with the introduction of several interacting policies of IEP, Volumetric Control, Dedicated Search Teams, Mandatory Drugs Testing, the replacement of phone cards, increased internal and perimeter security, and restrictions on temporary release. Prisoners emerged from this era with less property and fewer other privileges; and subject to much more thorough and frequent searches. In 1995, senior personnel within the high security estate within the Prison Service and the then Conservative Government were disillusioned with the so-called 'liberal-permissive paradigm' and set out explicitly to return power to staff. The political mandate was to provide 'decent but austere' regimes for prisoners[2]. There were other pressures contributing to the new penal landscape (see for example King 1999), some of which will be considered below.

---

2.   This was not an issue on which there was a consensus.

The work of the control project team included a review of existing best practice and experience and led to the Spurr Report (Prison Service 1996). The proposals for a new system of small units were intended to meet minimum standards and resist legal challenge. Their work was influenced by the publication of the Learmont Report in 1995 and by its recommendation (amongst others) that a Supermax facility be considered as a long term solution to the difficulties of managing seriously disruptive prisoners[3]. The Learmont Report had recommended a Control Prison for 200 prisoners, half of whom were thought to be in need of psychiatric attention. Learmont also recommended a Special Security Prison also for 200 prisoners – with some overlap between the two populations. Shortly after publication of the Learmont recommendations, the number of exceptional risk Category A prisoners requiring special security accommodation began to decline dramatically, owing to the repatriation of Irish prisoners as part of the emerging Northern Ireland peace process. At the time of writing (May 2000), the number of exceptional risk prisoners has fallen to fewer than ten.

The Spurr Report recommended that, pending the outcome of the Supermax project, the hard-core of seriously disruptive prisoners should be managed in a coordinated system of five close supervision units with graded regimes (opened as 'centres'), which would replace the existing CRC units and the Continuous Assessment Scheme which had grown up around it. This revised small unit system would cater for 60 prisoners. This was thought to be a realistic estimate without creating expensive specialist places that were not used. The principles underlying the CSCs were felt by the Project team to be appropriate to the management of disruptive prisoners whether as part of a small unit system or as part of a Supermax prison. The CSC system opened in 1998. It currently caters for 40 of the most difficult prisoners in the prison system in England and Wales. Its operation has not been straight-forward and some important problems, some of them long-standing, but others of them new, have arisen.

This paper addresses five questions arising from the operation of the centres to date. First, is it possible to identify a philosophy underpinning their creation? Secondly, what was the case for the introduction of a strict regime close supervision system, particularly given the prior negative experience of an arguably similar Control Unit in the 1970s? Thirdly, how did the policy of incentives and earned privileges, introduced nationally just before the creation of the new centres, apply in this part of the estate and to what effect? Fourthly, to what extent is the strategy that arose in practice a reflection of the report that created the centres – and what accounts for any departures? Finally, what is the meaning and significance of this development in the English penal landscape?

---

3. The renewed emphasis on rule following in the debate over the future of Strict Supervision units also influenced the shaping of the CSCs.

These are difficult questions, and the answers to them offered here are exploratory and necessarily partial. This account is based on a very limited amount of fieldwork, involving observation and interviewing of prisoners and staff in HMP Woodhill (two conducted jointly with a psychiatrist on the project team), attendance at research and Steering Group meetings, informal discussions with staff on A–D wings, and observation and attendance at staff meetings. It draws on several interviews carried our with senior personnel at Prison Service Headquarters, some access to official documentation, a brief review of the literature and experience from related research projects on small units for difficult prisoners (Bottomley, Liebling and Sparks 1994), incentives and earned privileges (Liebling, Muir, Rose and Bottoms 1997) and staff-prisoner relationships in a maximum security prison (Liebling and Price 1999). The issues raised became more complex as time went on. In this sense, the present paper constitutes 'unfinished business'.

2. Who are difficult prisoners?

It is impossible and unwise to consider the experiences of the CSCs without at least briefly reflecting on the population living in them. 'Difficult prisoners' are identified operationally by their placement in special locations – on the continuous assessment scheme, in segregation units on GOAD over very long periods of time, and in small units[4]. The labelling of a prisoner as 'difficult' normally occurs at a time when options for handling or management within the mainstream have been exhausted. Associated with the description 'difficult' is likely to be a history of indiscipline reports, violence or subversive activity and lengthy periods out of circulation (SPS 1990). Taken together, prisoners described as 'difficult' have been found to differ significantly from the normal long-term prisoner population on a number of variables including number of transfers and higher levels of violence (Williams and Longley 1987). They are prisoners who have persistently and seriously caused disruption. They may be hostage takers, serious drug dealers, general non-compliers, or serious assaulters of staff and other prisoners. As a proportion of the total prison population, they constitute a very small group (.08%, defined narrowly; a far smaller proportion than in most other jurisdictions) – but their behaviour can be seen as a continuum. As a proportion of the high security estate, they are still a small group (40/3500; or 1.1%). Those 'just beneath them' in terms of behaviour are normally managed in dispersals (because staffing levels are high, and if they pose serious difficulties in lower security prisons they tend to be upgraded) and in segregation units. The English prison service's most difficult group includes one murderer of a member of prison staff (a workshop instructor), four murderers of prisoners (1 twice), and several prisoners who have seriously assaulted other prisoners and staff. Some exert a 'malign and destructive influence' on establishments, even from within segregated environments (Coid 1998). These prisoners often cannot be safely contained within a therapeutic setting.

The question of what motivates disruptive prisoners is extraordinarily complex (for an excellent review, see Coid 1998). As individuals they are often articulate, insightful, talented and (perhaps sporadically) capable of reason. The following prisoner gave an extraordinary account of his prison career, observing often that 'it might have turned out differently'. He started his prison life 'terrified', but learned to fight back when 'certain inmates tried to take the piss out of me':

---

4. A study carried out by Williams and Longley on identifying 'difficult' prisoners in dispersal prisons found considerable disagreement over nomination for the term difficult. One key symptom was the number of establishments in which the sentence had been served (Williams and Longley 1987; 1989).

I thought, I'm going to have to do something. And because of the type of person that I am, if I'm going to do something, it has to be something serious. I'd always been that way. But it's not only that. Once you've done something like that..you've got to understand the culture as well.. and especially with being a black boy, this bad boy image, so you know, it's trying to live up to something you ain't really, you're only a kid, but you're trying to live up to an image, that is not you. But over a period of time that image becomes you, and you become that horrible person and you don't even realise you're a horrible person until you sit back and think, what am I doing. It's only then you realise. By that time.. it's never too late.. but by that time, certain norms come into your behaviour and your mannerisms, it's become normal to you, and you don't even realise it. For instance – this is when I knew that there was something wrong with me, something dramatically wrong with me. I was in [previous prison], and I was standing in the kitchen doing a bit of cooking. I'll never forget this, this is when I knew I had to something about myself, to try and have some sort of humanity within myself. Uhm, don't know what the problem was but obviously there was problems between some people, one of the people in the kitchen was having problems with other inmates, they had this hot fat, all day they had this hot fat boiling. This other person bent down, two people came at him, poured boiling hot fat over him, started cooking him alive. Now his ears fell off, his eyes bulged out, his nose fell off, do you know, I didn't even flicker, I didn't even bat an eyelid, it was like nothing, that's when I knew something was wrong with me, I'd got no feelings towards that...you know? (prisoner)

Such prisoners can be implausibly defended (a wing always 'got burned down', someone 'got hit', people 'get moved'); there is very little responsibility for action, in between these flashes of insight. They can be volatile, violent and aggressive. Their language is punctuated with words like 'honour' and 'fairness', whilst their behaviour is impulsive and destructive in the extreme. They have no trust in the authorities who confine them – and generating any sustainable level of trust is extremely difficult. They recreate punitive environments and have a fine sensitivity to acts of indifference. Some seem to challenge or dare those responsible for their management to treat them evenly in the face of what they can throw at them. Many fit the descriptions of borderline personality disorder offered by Coid (1991; 1998) or the definition of 'personality disorder', often specified as untreatable or dangerous (Coid 1998). They are emotionally and behaviourally volatile and may be narcissistic with 'an aggressive sense of entitlement' (Coid 1998: 433). Three types of difficult prisoners were identified by the Control Review Committee (Home Office 1984): those who behaved in a disorderly fashion themselves; those who encouraged others to misbehave; and those who suffered from a form of mental disturbance. Many cross these categories. Other groups may include prisoners requiring or seeking protection; and 'problem personality' prisoners who may be highly unpredictable and unstable but do not attract a psychiatric diagnosis (Coid 1998). Some are of course, wrongly labelled, but others are not. Some have been on the receiving end of brutalising experiences in prison as well as at the centre of violence and disruption. Many commentators on special provision for difficult prisoners underestimate (or fail to mention) the nature and extent of the difficulties involved.

3.   The management of disruptive prisoners in the UK

> The policy of giving very long sentences up to and including the full life of a prisoner introduces a new type of imprisonment, bringing with it human problems which will have to be faced (Home Office 1966: 5).

The question of the appropriate management of a disruptive minority within the long-term prison system has been the subject of debate for several decades. The appropriate handling of this group has been a prerequisite for the maintenance of an arguably quite liberal and thoughtful approach to the management of the more compliant majority of long-term prisoners (see Bottoms and Light 1987). The existing dispersal system (renamed the High Security Estate in 1998) was established in 1968 following the recommendations of Sir Leon Radzinowicz and his Sub-Committee of the Advisory Council on the Penal System following a number of high profile escapes from Wandsworth and Wormwood Scrubs in 1964 and 1966 respectively. These escapes led to an inquiry (Report of the Inquiry into Prison Escapes and Security) carried out by Lord Mountbatten (Home Office 1966). The Report recommended the introduction of a system of security classification, more careful inspection of prisons, and the building of a new maximum security prison, Vectis, which was to be located on the Isle of Wight and which was to house those prisoners thought most likely to try to escape or whose escape would be most dangerous to the pubic or the security of the State. The Advisory Council's Report on *The Regime for Long-Term Prisoners in Conditions of Maximum Security*, conducted under the chairmanship of Leon Radzinowicz, rejected Mountbatten's arguments for concentration of this 'hard core' largely in recognition of the problems that could be caused by creating a single option, last resort concentration of the most difficult prisoners in one place:

> During the course of its inquiry the Sub-Committee became increasingly doubtful about the possibility of establishing a satisfactory regime within a fortress-type prison in which all maximum security prisoners were concentrated (Home Office 1968: v).

Their concerns included the danger that 'the atmosphere might become repressive', the difficulties of identifying with any degree of accuracy the selection of a group requiring the highest levels of security, and the adverse effect that such an establishment might have on 'the general respect in which the service was held by the community and on recruitment to it' (p. 15). The Council recognised that 'the arguments are finely balanced', but felt that the balance of advantage lay in establishing a policy of dispersal whereby a small proportion of Category A prisoners, many but not all of whom were difficult to control, would be located in a slightly larger number of establishments which could therefore achieve a more 'liberal regime within a secure perimeter'. This more liberal regime would only be possible if some alternative provision were made for the 'disruptive minority' who would make such a policy untenable. Prisoners who could not be controlled by a liberal and constructive regime would be housed (for a time) in small segregation units within the grounds of the main prison, but with its own staff and with additional control and restrictions on movements. The regime of a dispersal prison was to combine security with humanity, was to be delivered by mature and experienced staff, and was to incorporate the principles of self-respect, choice, participation, variety, movement and the earning of privileges (pp. 28–28), within a context of reasonable conditions:

> We do not mean by this that the regime should be based on an automatic system of rewards for outward conformity, and punishments for all minor breaches of the rules laid down for the outwardly smooth running of the institution. Such a regime does not increase self-respect. We mean rather that the aim should be to create an atmosphere within the prison that will make the prisoner wish to earn for himself improvements in the conditions of his existence. The prisoner can earn these by work. We shall suggest, for example, that prisoners should have better clothes, but they should make a contribution towards the cost out of the earnings of their work... The prisoner should also be able to earn the opportunities for greater variety in his daily and yearly routine by his response to his fellow prisoners and to the efforts of the staff (Home Office 1968: 30).

The policy of dispersal was adopted by the new Home Secretary, James Callaghan, in 1968. Seven establishments were selected for adaptation: Albany, Gartree, Parkhurst, Wakefield, Wormwood Scrubs D Wing and Long Lartin (which was being built at the time) and Hull in 1971. A further new prison (Full Sutton) would also become a dispersal establishment when it was built in the future. After serious disturbances at Albany and Gartree in 1972, the dispersal policy was reviewed and the number of establishments increased (to include Frankland). A number of other modifications were made, intended to strengthen the system, including larger segregation units in each prison, some restrictions on the numbers of prisoners allowed to congregate together at one time, other security and control procedures and increased staffing levels. Two new facilities were introduced: a control unit with a strict regime at Wakefield (two were planned but the second was never used) and short term secure accommodation in selected local prisons for troublesome prisoners from dispersals who could be transferred at short notice under what was then Rule 43 for a 'cooling off' period. The transfer of disruptive prisoners to local prisons for 'cooling off' periods (CI 10/74; revised in 1990 as CI 37), although clearly contentious (see Sparks et al. 1996), was welcomed by Governors and is still used often, under fresh terms.

The control unit at Wakefield was opened in 1974 following the report of a Home Office Working Party on Dispersal and Control. It was based on an intentionally austere staging system, each stage lasting 60, extended to 90 days[5]. In 1981 the courts held that the regime contravened the Prison Rules only in so far as it did not provide for prisoners' placement in the unit to be reviewed every 28 days (Williams v Home Office 1981). The regime was severely criticised by prisoners and was bitterly and legally challenged. The CRC Report described the unsuccessful Wakefield regime as an 'obstacle course' and a 'blind alley', which was 'not in keeping with the values we now try to instil in our training' (p. 17). The unit housed a total of six men in its short life. It was closed in 1975 on the grounds that it had not been used to the expected extent and was wasteful of staff resources and accommodation.

The case against dispersal was considered again following a serious disturbance at Hull in 1976 and in the May Report of 1979. Both the Chief Inspector's Inquiry into the disturbances at Hull and the May Inquiry concluded that the concept of dispersal was satisfactory, but its administration could be improved. There was a recognition that control problem prisoners were not all Category A. In 1980, in response to growing concerns about breakdowns in control, another Working Group on Control in Dispersal Prisons was set up. In 1983, following further serious disturbances in dispersal prisons and new restrictions on parole eligibility for certain long term prisoners, and in response to a request that the Group's work be accelerated, it was reconstituted as the Control Review Committee, with new terms of reference and a revised membership. The Control Review Committee were to recommend the experimental and innovative system of small units for difficult prisoners whose apparent failure immediately preceded the establishment of the Close Supervision Centres. It is worth looking briefly at the principles and operation of these units, and at their successes and failures, in order to explore the context in which the current CSC system was devised.

The Control Review Committee recognised that although there was no satisfactory alternative[6], the present dispersal system accentuated 'the inherent tension between security and control', by placing many prisoners in conditions that were more secure than they required. This policy achieved satisfactory results in terms of the number of escapes (there were very few), but placed a damaging level of strain on the atmosphere of each establishment. The aim should remain to aspire to an open regime in each of the existing dispersals:

---

5. At Stage 1, the prisoner did not associate with other prisoners, except for one hour's exercise per day. At Stage 2, prisoners were allowed to associate during work, educational and leisure activities. Prisoners could return to normal location after 180 days if they demonstrated 'sustained good behaviour and constructive effort in the unit'. Failure to cooperate led to a return to Stage 1.

6. Whilst current physical designs were in place. The CRC Report speculates that new generation prison design might make the concentration option more attractive in the future (Home Office 1984: 3).

We, too, believe that this approach is right both on humanitarian grounds and, in so far as an open regime reduces tension between staff and inmates, on control grounds. By an 'open regime' we certainly do not mean one that allows prisoners to decide what to do from day to day, but one that offers a range of constructive activities, the opportunity of association, and supervision by staff who have the time and training to take a personal interest in each inmate as an individual. We are sure that this is best achieved within a framework of rules that are applied firmly and fairly (Home Office 1984: 5).

Their report argued that control was difficult to achieve in this way (that is, in large units with a relatively open regime) and that several improvements could be made to the existing dispersal system. These improvements included slower entry into a dispersal prison after sentencing, a recognition that the dispersal regime was not suitable for all long-term prisoners, clearer incentives and disincentives to good and bad behaviour, more centrally administered allocation and a more flexible system for managing the most difficult prisoners. They recommended the establishment of a system of small units to be created outside the dispersal estate to provide longer-term relief for the mainstream system. The whole system should:

...[B]e structured in a way which encourages him to co-operate rather then the reverse and which makes a clear connection between the prisoner's behaviour and the course of his prison career (Home Office 1984: 8).

They identified contradictions in the current system whereby persistently disruptive behaviour could secure transfer to a more desirable location, whilst good behaviour could secure transfer to a lower security prison in undesirable locations where facilities were relatively sparse. They reconsidered the staging system attempted in the Wakefield control unit and at other points in penal practice:

We share the view that it is essential to provide a coherent, progressive career for long-term prisoners within a framework which makes a direct connection between privilege and behaviour; but we doubt whether a staged system of the kind suggested is the best way to achieve this. When such systems have been tried in the past they have proved to have serious short-comings in practice. Both the old 'stage' system for adult prisoners (which was abolished in 1967) and the 'grade' system for Borstal trainees (which finally came to an end in 1982) fell into disrepute because there was an inevitable tendency for progress through the stages to become automatic and for delays to be exceptional and related only to specific acts of indiscipline. The practical difficulties of drawing up an adequate scale for measuring institutional behaviour, and assessing such concepts as whether a prisoner was trying to improve his general attitude, proved overwhelming (Home Office 1984: 10).

They also pointed out that such a system, if location-based, would end up with all the most difficult prisoners concentrated in one place, and for long periods; and that the ability to separate particular prisoners (for example gang members, or sworn enemies) would be limited. They suggested instead that a system of sentence or individual 'prison career' planning based on thorough assessment and prisoners' own participation could offer the sort of meaningful progression they envisaged. For those who could not cope with an open and progressive structure, and for whom existing measures were inadequate, a new system of long-term small units should be devised:

> These units – which we shall call long-term prisoner units – will provide relief for the mainstream long-term prisons. To that extent, and to that extent only, they have the same aim as the control unit experiment of 1974–75. But we are emphatically not advocating any return to the kind of regime which the control unit operated (Home Office 1984: 16–17).

The Committee assumed that if the whole package of recommendations were implemented, and a serious attempt made to make the long-term prison system more consistent and 'psychologically credible', fewer difficult prisoners would emerge. A system of small units was a reasonable alternative to long-term segregation:

> [W]e would expect small units to provide an environment in which staff can exercise more effective supervision as well as becoming more closely involved with prisoners than is possible in a normal large dispersal prison wing, and in which inmates can receive more individual attention and support (Home Office 1987: 13).

The CRC's recommendations were welcomed as 'a positive agenda for establishing a better framework of control on our long-term prison system' (Home Office 1987: 7). They were accepted, some further improvements to the dispersal system were made (including this time a reduction in the overall size of the estate), and a system of small units was devised broadly along the lines the CRC envisaged, as developed by the Research and Advisory Group. The regimes were varied and included one unit for prisoners deemed unstable but not suitable for transfer under the Mental Health Act, one unit with a high degree of structure and staff involvement, and one with less structure and some psychological assistance to prisoners[7]. There were five principles underlying the establishment of the CRC system:

- They were not punitive in purpose;
- They were not to be regarded as places of last resort;
- The units were to complement each other;
- There was to be openness about the establishment and operation of the units;
- Participation in activities was to be voluntary.

The aim of the units was to help prisoners who were oscillating between wings and segregation units to find ways of coping in smaller, more supportive situations and then guide them back into the mainstream, or test them gradually in situations offering more freedom (Home Office 1984: p. 22). The Research and Advisory Group established to provide advice on the coordination and evaluation of the proposed units (and other core subjects relevant to order and control) saw them as 'an alternative environment in which prisoners will have the opportunity to find new ways of coping with imprisonment and relating to staff' (Home Office 1987: para 42). The conditions in the units were to be, as far as possible, similar to those in normal long-term prisons:

> [T]hat is, the range of permitted privileges and possessions should be similar to those allowed in dispersal prisons; a full programme of constructive activities (including work, education, PE and recreation) should be available; and inmates should spend the majority of the day out of their cell (Home Office 1987: 14).

There would be a high degree of involvement of staff. Participation in the activities offered was to be voluntary, as one way of reducing conflict between staff and prisoners and allowing for the development of constructive relationships. The question of whether or not a prisoner's consent was required for *transfer* into a unit was addressed in some detail by RAG. Some prisoners would welcome the opportunity to break the cycle of misbehaviour; others would resist cooperation. Legally, consent was not required for transfer into the units. After some deliberation, the Group decided:

> We are sure that there is much to be said for trying to enlist the prisoner's interest in being transferred to a special unit and we think that for certain kinds of regime (for

7. The two other regimes recommended but never introduced were a more specialist unit devised on more explicitly psychological principles; and one with a sociological and social psychological dimension, similar in nature to Barlinnie but with clearer boundaries (Home Office 1987: 42–43; Bottoms 1992; and see Bottomley, Liebling and Sparks 1994).

example, a social learning regime) this might be particularly desirable. But, we recognise that the units will not be able to play their part in the management of the most difficult and disruptive prisoners if such prisoners are given a choice as to whether they transfer to a special unit or not (Home Office 1987: 39).

It was recognised that the small unit structure would not cater for all difficult prisoners, but it was hoped that they would relieve the mainstream of its most persistent and serious cases (p. 26). Whilst prisoners could be deselected after an initial assessment period, they could be held in units without their consent if there were 'good reasons' to do so. Decisions were made by a Special Units Selection Committee, consisting of interested Headquarters parties and staff and managers of the units.

Only three such units (increasingly referred to as Special Units) were in operation at any one time at Parkhurst (opened in 1985), Lincoln (opened in 1987), Hull (in 1988) and later, Woodhill (which replaced Lincoln in 1993), although as mentioned above, others were intended but never opened (see Home Office 1987; Bottomley 1995). The policy of 'no consent', whilst publicly defended, proved impossible to operate in practice mainly due to the open nature of the small unit regimes. This was despite strenuous attempts made by members of SUSC and unit staff and managers to motivate and encourage individual prisoners to cooperate. Prisoners referred to but not selected for the units were often turned down 'because they did not meet the criteria', but officially recorded explanations underplay the extent to which deselection was linked to potential and actual disruption in the open regimes obtaining in the units (personal communication).

Around 22 prisoners were housed in the CRC units in 1996 – a much lower figure than originally envisaged. The maximum number held in the units at any one time was 35 (Bottomley 1995). The units did not replace but supplemented the internal and short-term strategies already in place and there remained (according to the Spurr Report) a core of prisoners who were 'too disruptive' for the CRC units (some had been transferred but were deselected because of their behaviour). These prisoners (an increasing number, at around 23 in 1996), remained on a Continuous Assessment Scheme – something that was not envisaged by CRC:

> The Continuous Assessment Scheme was created in response to the fact that dispersals were disillusioned with CRCs; they didn't work. They had legitimacy in the eyes of prisoners but none in the eyes of dispersal governors. The CAS came about as a way of legitimising the system. It reinforced to prisons the fact that they have to apply the formal strategies outlined in CI 28/93 – any transfer had to be formally

authorised from the centre. It placed an onus on the owning prison to convene proper case conferences. It tried to formalise some of the best practices and processes, and reduce the use of 28 day lie downs (Senior manager).

A comparison of the profiles of CRC and CAS prisoners showed that prisoners on CAS were responsible for higher numbers of assaults on staff, and may have been slightly disproportionately non-white, and convicted of robbery (Spurr 1996: Annex E), but in many respects they were similar to the CRC population. CAS prisoners were transferred at regular intervals between establishments in the hope that some environments might facilitate more stable behaviour than others, and that at the very least, the control problem was being shared. The scheme (a more formal version of what already happened in practice) was managed centrally from 1993 (Circular Instruction 28/93) in order to give more legitimacy to a system that did not seem to remove or manage successfully those prisoners who posed the greatest difficulties to dispersal prisons. Part of the aim of the formal CAS system was to centrally select more prisoners suitable for the CRC units where possible and to make what had developed as a rather 'underground' process of frequent transfer, more visible:

> We made sure we didn't over-burden one given establishment and could move prisoners into appropriate prisons depending on their security category. In some cases it was successful because we had that flexibility and could put prisoners where you would never think of putting them and Governors would be reassured and prepared to accept them because they had an underwritten guarantee that if it went wrong we would get rid of the prisoners for them so they were prepared to give the prisoners a chance, where in earlier days they wouldn't have been; we gave them a three month guarantee (Senior manager).

Whilst the above CRC/CAS 'small units plus' strategy for managing difficult prisoners had many strengths, including the provision of varied regimes including one semi-psychiatric unit, the provision of relief to the mainstream, some modest returns to normal location and the apparently successful management of disruptive behaviour in the Special Units, with a significant reduction in assaults and violence, there were a number of serious difficulties. Segregation units in dispersal prisons were full, the system did not remove those prisoners who orchestrated problems but were not fully active (the subversive[8]), referral to CRCs was long-winded so that governors of dispersals had reservations about its usefulness to them and the regimes in them could be seen as 'rewarding', compared to long-term segregation (although not by comparison with ordinary dispersal locations). The regimes lacked the variety and focus originally envisaged (see Bottomley et al. 1994), and in practice they

---

8. A category of 'dangerous prisoner' given some attention in the Radzinowicz Report (p.16; para. 40).

required the consent – or at least the cooperation – of prisoners. A small number of prisoners moved between units rather than from a unit back into the mainstream and a larger number 'failed' to return to mainstream conditions but returned to the Continuous Assessment Scheme. There was little incentive or scope for establishments to work with these disruptive prisoners if they were continually on the move. All disruptive prisoners had periods of stability interspersed with periods of serious violence or disruption. Sometimes these periods of stability occurred on normal location. There was, in Toch's words, a 'person-environment transaction' about which little was systematically known (Toch and Adams 1989). The very expensive CRC system[9] provided some limited relief to long-term prisons but was not – in the eyes of those managing and requiring it – a satisfactory way of managing difficult prisoners[10]. It partially fulfilled one main objective – to 'provide relief for the mainstram long-term prisons' (Home Office 1994: 16) and did:

[P]rovide an alternative location for over 100 long-term prisoners who posed persistent control problems, but whose behaviour during their stays in one or more of the special units...has normally shown a significant reduction in aggression towards prison staff and other prisoners. Thus the aim of 'maintaining control' within the special units, in a generally safe and humane environment, appears to have been achieved for the majority of prisoners for most of the time (Bottomley 1995: 45).

That so few prisoners were referred, and so few of those referred accepted, was, however, a major weakness. Its objectives in relation to 'guiding prisoners back into the mainstream' were also less successfully met. The regimes in the CRC units had converged and lost focus, and staff complained about high stress levels and unsatisfactory working conditions. The increasing pressure on segregation unit places reflected an underlying problem in the operation of regimes for long-term prisoners, which a revised small units strategy should help to address.

9. The cost based on real occupancy levels in 1995/6 was £85,000 per prisoner per year. This was largely because of under-occupancy, which was a continual problem with CRC Units. The equivalent cost of a special hospital place was £69,000.
10. The criteria by which difficult prisoners were referred to a CRC and/or management under CAS were a history of disruptive and aggressive behaviour, violence to staff and/or prisoners, have regularly incurred disciplinary reports, have caused serious damage to prison property, have shown dangerous behaviour (such as rooftop protests, hostage taking), have a history of mental abnormality and have failed to respond to earlier strategies to improve control (IG 28/93: para 24).

4.

The case for a strict regime unit

We made all the mistakes you can make with this population. The way it was set up, it fed the prisoners' egos. Staff were too flexible. The word 'Special' was a major mistake. Asking staff to change their whole culture of dealing with prisoners was our biggest mistake. Prisoners fooled us. At the first sign of disagreement, whatever the progress, they reverted to type. We thought we could change the world. Prisoners could make perverse demands. Every time it went wrong, we'd have a clear out. We'd be left with one or two prisoners. There was no framework. In a way, IEP showed it up. This scheme tries to prevent staff getting sucked in. It tries to address the things we didn't get right: structure, activity, accountability, and staff power and confidence. (Senior manager)

The case was made by the Spurr Report for a strict regime unit on the grounds that the relatively open CRC unit regimes had in practice required prisoners' consent and had thereby excluded or deselected prisoners guilty of especially recalcitrant behaviour. A strict regime would provide a deterrent, was compatible with the recently introduced incentives and earned privileges strategy, would link progress more clearly to behaviour and would provide an opportunity for assessment (Prison Service 1996). There were concerns, particularly in the light of experience with the Wakefield Control Unit, that such a regime (and the prisoners subjected to it) would become negatively labelled, that some would regard admission as a 'badge of honour', that violent and unstable behaviour would be exacerbated, that prisoners would remain for long periods, that there would be high levels of pressure and stress for staff, and that litigation would ensue (Prison Service 1996: 15–16). Much more attention was paid to the avoidance of legal challenge, with the careful drafting of operational standards. All of these concerns were, however, to prove well founded. The distinction between a *strict* regime (designed to contain and modify behaviour) and a *punitive* regime (designed to punish it) was a fine (some would argue meaningless) one. The Spurr Report argued that:

Strictness in this sense thus avoids punishment – not merely because of the intentions of the administrator but because it acts as a 'modifier' suggesting restraint and control extending further than is usually necessary in order materially to attract and engage the attention of the offending prisoner. A prisoner unable or unwilling to respond to the obligations and inducements of social engagements is invited to take a hand in his own betterment through the betterment of his own environment (Prison Service 1996: 16).

A *utilitarian* rather than *moral* motivation to comply was assumed (see McConville 1995). Transfer to the unit would be justified on the grounds that the presenting disruptive behaviour was being addressed. A restricted and a structured regime was envisaged, which would not require the consent of prisoners, and whose aim would be to contain and change disruptive behaviour. In order to avoid becoming punitive and to prevent prisoners becoming 'cause celebres', prisoners should be regularly reviewed and assessed, interaction with staff should be maintained, and prisoners should be 'given the opportunity and encouragement to progress' (Prison Service 1996: 17). There was also acknowledgment in the Report that non-compliance was a motivator (or means of survival) for some prisoners.

The purpose, aims and principles of the revised system were as follows.

> Close Supervision Centres operate as part of a national management strategy which aims to secure the return of problematic or disruptive prisoners to a settled and acceptable pattern of behaviour. The functions of CSCs are:
>
> - to remove the most seriously disruptive prisoners from mainstream dispersal/training prisons;
>
> - to contain highly dangerous or disruptive individuals in small, highly supervised units with safety for staff and prisoners;
>
> - to provide opportunity for individuals to address their antisocial disruptive behaviour in a controlled environment;
>
> - to stabilise behaviour and prepare individuals for a successful return to the mainstream or long-term containment in designated units.

The intended aim of the CSC system 'is explicitly to manage disruptive prisoners in conditions of safety for staff and other prisoners and to provide encouragement and opportunity for them to change their behaviour. It is explicitly not aiming to punish' (p. 66). Behavioural change and long-term containment were regarded as the necessarily dual aims of the system. Its core operating principles included a framework of incentives and earned privileges, formally published procedures and reasons for allocation, a coordinated set of regimes, no consent required, formal assessment and review, active staff engagement, avoidance of 'drift' and 'conditioning' and external audit. Prisoners would begin in a structured regime and would be able to progress (to one of a range of intervention units) or regress (to the restricted regime) depending on their behaviour. Each unit should have a clear and stated aim. The restricted regime was to 'manage prisoners whose behaviour has been so challenging and disruptive that strict conditions of segregation are necessary to protect staff and prisoners'; to 'encourage a settled pattern of acceptable behaviour'; and to monitor, assess and review. Subject to a favourable risk assessment, prisoners who stabilised in this regime could be transferred to the structured unit. On the restricted regime, privileges would be restricted to the basic level[11]; association was not available and specialist psychological assistance would be available for staff support and individual prisoner assessment. There would be no prisoner participation in the running of the unit. The structured regime provided some opportunity to participate in association, in constructive activities and behaviour programmes. There would still be no prisoner participation in the running of the unit and settled behaviour on this unit would lead to transfer to an intervention unit. The level of privileges would still be basic. Only when prisoners reached one of a small range of intervention units would privileges reach the standard level. There would be more opportunities, more staff involvement and less structure on these units, as well as some consultation with prisoners about the operation of the units. No prisoner would be able to stay on the non-psychiatric intervention unit for more than three years.

This scheme was intended to provide clear incentives for progression, with an additional limited number of high control cells for the very few whose behaviour became so exceptionally dangerous that they threatened the operation of the unit. Prisoners would begin in the structured regime (unless exceptionally dangerous) and then progress either

---

11. A brief description of privileges:

A Wing – (Restricted) Basic. Prisoners were entitled to 2 half hour visits a month (which could be taken together). They took meals in their cells. They were entitled to radios (none accepted) and could exercise in pairs (again, at the time of the research, prisoners were not taking this up). They had no association. They were entitled to writing and drawing materials. They could make phone calls. They spent limited private cash (£2.50) via canteen order forms. Prisoners were unlocked one at a time, with an SO and 5 officers. There were very formal and limited relations between staff and prisoners ('studied indifference').

B Wing – (Structured) Assessment and Induction. Standard Prisoners were entitled to 2 one hour visits per month; to £5 private cash; and they could earn up to £8 cleaning. Prisoners associated in groups of 3 (but there was no evening association). They wore prison clothes. They were entitled to a shower every other day and to association up to 3 days per week. They were able to see education staff.

C Wing – (Intervention). Standard. £10 private cash and prisoners were employed and could earn up to £10.50. Prisoners could wear their own clothes. They could have tapes and CDs and there was electric power in cells. Prisoners were entitled to 3 or 4 one hour visits per month. Staff ran ETS, and psychologists saw individual prisoners on a one-to-one basis. Association took place one afternoon and three evenings per week. Staff spent a lot of time with prisoners and did regular assessments (2 staff members carrying out long interviews usually at weekends).

D Wing – (Segregation). Basic. Prisoners were unlocked with an SO and 5 officers. They were entitled to 1 hour exercise, which was taken in pairs, in separate yards. They were searched before and after, with their hands above their heads. They had few visits, which took place in closed conditions (except legal visits). They were fed through hatches. They had no access to education; and limited access to the library. They could receive and write letters. Two prisoners were on C+R unlock. Staff were anxious that the regime had damaging effects on (particularly psychiatrically ill) prisoners.

upwards or downwards, according to their behaviour. Enhanced regime level privileges would not be available to prisoners within the CSC system, but only after 'a sustained period of good behaviour in the mainstream' (p. 31). The system offered more flexibility than the previous CRC units as 'Disruptive behaviour in the Intervention Units could result in a return to a structured regime rather than deselection and return to the mainstream' (ibid.). Movements up and down were to be carefully handled, and there was a distinction made between individual incidents of bad behaviour, which should be 'punished in the normal way', and a pattern of disruptive behaviour which may lead to downgrading (p. 63). Keeping prisoners on their units was seen as 'part of the strategy for working with disruptive behaviour'. The system would require 'careful management and monitoring' and sufficient incentives to move upwards and outwards were 'essential'. A need to keep this new system under review was explicitly stated in the report. There was a clear expectation that the revised system would, unlike the old CRC system, make the CAS obsolete.

To summarise, the CRC system had worked for only a limited number of prisoners. It had little legitimacy (or was of limited practical use) in the eyes of many governors working in dispersal prisons, as referral was cumbersome and prisoners often returned. By the time of its demise, regimes were vague and undifferentiated, the living conditions for prisoners had become unacceptably high, particularly in a punitive populist climate (Bottoms 1994), and prisoners were refusing to move out into ordinary locations. Its achievements were its multi-disciplinary approach (including dedicated education, probation and psychology contributions), the successes reported in the specialist psychiatric units, the flexibility in managing individuals and the dramatic lack of assaultive behaviour by prisoners located in them (see also Cooke 1989, on Barlinnie). These successes were linked to the fact that it was possible to develop relationships with prisoners and to engage morally with them, to some extent:

> One of its strengths was that you could find flexible solutions to individual problems. You could put in place very imaginative options. You could be creative. We wouldn't get away with many of the things we used to do, now (Senior manager).

The Spurr Report had devised a model that was intended to include and handle the most disruptive, uncooperative and subversive prisoners. It was intended to be 'more robust' than the liberal but arguably only partially effective CRC system and to cater for the most extreme cases. It had a dual containment and progressive function and was designed with a handful of the most intractable prisoners in mind. One of its key principles was that the mainstream system should look more attractive, so that the standard of privileges in the CSC system would never reach the level achievable in normal dispersal conditions. This was a major departure from the CRC principles and came about partly as a result of political pressure not to acknowledge publicly that there existed a handful of prisoners who 'could not be made safe':

> It wouldn't have been acceptable to come up with a model which allowed for that group [the most extreme], just because of their poor behaviour and unwillingness to conform with whatever system, that meant they would actually be moved back into a dispersal prison. It had to be a system that could be tested to destruction, so the concept it worked from was that bad behaviour would keep prisoners there and they would not progress. They would only progress if they behaved. That signal came from above, and the experiences of the CRC (Senior manager).

5.   The role of incentives and earned privileges (IEP)

As seen in several of the reports already mentioned, some attempt to 'send the right signals' and to link compliant or good behaviour with privileges has been made at many stages of penal practice, and in particular, in relation to long-term prisoners. A major distinction can be made, however, between approaches which focus on 'carrots', in the context of a high threshold quality of life (as in the CRC Report, the Woolf Report, and so on), and an approach emphasising the 'sticks', with a very low or austere threshold provision (as in the Wakefield Control Unit, the CSC system as devised, and some Basic Regimes in training and other prisons). One of the key policy decisions in the design of a new small unit structure concerned the setting of a maximum level of privileges which had to be lower than the maximum allowed in dispersal prisons, and a minimum level which was, even in comparison with some segregation units, very low indeed:

> The day I came I had my own clothes on, in the segregation at [X prison]. I came straight from the segregation. I had my own clothes on, I could spend £10 a week, I had all me photos, a few hundred of them, I had a big stereo, I could phone my family every day... I haven't been charged with no adjudication or nothing. They took it all off me and said you can earn it back. Well once they said that I said, well, you can keep it (CSC prisoner).

The Spurr Report had taken into account the need to make sure prisoners located in CSCs would not be given material incentives to remain there. The Report also took into account the recent judicial review of HMP Swaleside's Basic Regime, which had been adjudged too austere and insufficiently differentiated from a segregation unit and the experience of the Wakefield Control Unit. The CSC's structured and restricted regimes were therefore designed to be austere enough but consistent with IG 74/95 and beyond legal challenge. A different decision about what prisoners were entitled to might have been taken had the Spurr Report not coincided with the launch of a major national policy of incentives and earned privileges, again intended to 'rein in' privilege drift estate-wide, and gain control of appeasement practices and liberal interpretation of privilege entitlements in some establishments. Several senior managers observed that the CSC system would have made sense with an enhanced level of privileges available to prisoners who simply could not be handled in dispersal conditions.

A Home Office-funded evaluation of the IEP initiative was carried out by the Cambridge Institute of Criminology between May 1995 and July 1997. It aimed to evaluate the implementation and impact of the introduction of incentives-based regimes in a selected range of establishments (Liebling, Muir, Rose and Bottoms 1997). The national policy for IEP was introduced in July 1995. It sought formally 'to ensure that prisoners earn privileges by responsible behaviour and participation in hard work and other constructive activity'. Within this overall purpose, five main aims were identified:

(i)   to provide that privileges generally are earned by prisoners through good behaviour and performance and are removable if prisoners fail to maintain acceptable standards;

(ii)   to encourage responsible behaviour by prisoners;

(iii)   to encourage hard work and other constructive activity by prisoners;

(iv)   to encourage sentenced prisoners' progress through the prison system; and

(v)   to create a more disciplined, better controlled and safer environment for prisoners and staff.

The policy had other aims, which were to do with achieving consistency across the estate, and reducing the quality of life of those prisoners who failed to comply. The policy was a complex and significant one, but it was introduced quickly and with no training for staff. The Instruction to Governors 74/1995 was not fully implemented in the five prisons studied at the time of the research (which included one dispersal prison). Major differences were found between establishments in the extent of implementation. Formal procedures were under-developed in most of the research establishments, leaving prisoners disgruntled and establishments vulnerable to legal challenge. Important differences appeared between prisons in use of the policy. For example, the five prisons varied widely in their use of the Basic regime (the lowest level of privileges, regarded as a punishment) in terms of numbers, criteria and in regime provision. This was linked to other systematic differences between establishments (including for example, the perceived aims of the IEP policy, but also the nature and extent of control problems in each establishment, the quality of staff-prisoner relationships, and the perceived compliance of the prisoner population). The policy was implemented and used most carefully in the dispersal prison. This was related to perceived adverse prisoner reaction to the policy and careful hands-on senior management oversight of process issues. Prisoners regarded the principles of IEP as fair, but thought it was often operated unfairly. They considered they had insufficiently clear ideas about what behaviour was required, and did not fully understand the appeals procedures.

Staff, on the other hand, approved of IEP and thought of it as a useful tool, allowing them to handle problems with individual prisoners, and to do so quickly. Prisoners recognised the importance of the policy, and the power given to staff in operating it. The research found overall, however, that IEP did not result in significant improvements to prisoner behaviour. Instead, it seemed to result (along with other policies introduced at the time) to losses on prisoners' perceptions of the legitimacy of prison regimes, and in the quality of staff-prisoner relationships (which are, in turn, both related to the maintenance of order, IEP's main aim). Despite these specific results, IEP did become an important tool in the Prison Service's drive to improve order, to make prison a constructive experience and to strengthen the role of staff. Prisoner behaviour was, as expected, more complex than suggested by the 'simple' optimising model of IEP. The research suggested that the legal framework within which IEP is intended to operate as a policy required greater emphasis. It also needed to be dovetailed more effectively with sentence planning and personal officer schemes; and constructive activities. The research did result in a re-issuing of a revised Instruction to Governors (currently being piloted). This new Instruction does emphasise the legal framework of the policy, the importance of process, and the flexibility needed to make it work effectively in the management (or motivation) of individual prisoners.

The outcome effects of IEP were different between Time 1 and Time 2 for some prisoner groups. The most important were:

(i)   level of education: those with no educational qualifications responded more favourably to IEP[12];
(ii)   type of offence: drug offenders who were not current drug users responded more favourably towards IEP;
(iii) age: older offenders expressed more negative attitudes towards IEP and showed an increase in misbehaviour; and
(iv)   vulnerability: prisoners more at risk of suicide showed a greater drop in perceptions of fairness than other prisoners.

The findings on vulnerability were significant and correlated with related research findings about prisoners with high need levels and their negative perceptions of staff fairness. The higher the vulnerability, the greater the drop in perceptions of staff fairness between Time 1 (before the policy was introduced) and Time 2. It was clear from this and the supporting interviews that 'bad behaviour' and 'vulnerable behaviour' were sometimes confused (and might overlap). The relationship between 'offending behaviour' and 'destructive behaviour' and staff responses to these behaviours was in need of attention.

12. We interpreted the findings on educational qualifications (inferentially and therefore tentatively) in terms of locus of control theory. Those with high external locus of control tended to respond more favourably to IEP (and external mode of behaviour control).

In the final research report, we identified three main areas of concern which seemed to account for the lack of positive impact on prisoner behaviour. These were (i) organisational issues, such as the limited availability of rewards, difficulties in administering the scheme correctly and fairly, lack of clarity about what 'good behaviour' in the prisons context might be, and lack of attention to *normative* as opposed to purely instrumental motives to compliance; (ii) the complexity of prisoner behaviour and motivation, which may include many other variables besides material reward (socialisation, legitimation); and (iii) the specific problems of persistent misbehaviour. Research suggests that for some prisoners the 'reward' of confronting and resisting authority far exceeds the material rewards available in prison, so that issues of personal identity and autonomy require prisoners to seek such intangible rewards; not all behaviour is rational, and many prisoners become trapped in 'destructive interactions' with their environment. Persistently troublesome prisoners may be especially likely to define their environment as hostile or rejecting, and may feel urged to respond in less than 'optimising' ways.

Our results suggested that whilst IEP had led to significantly greater staff control, it had also led to the wide use of discretion. Perceptions of unfairness by prisoners offset most of the expected improvements in behaviour.

These results were not available at the time of the opening of the CSC units. There were difficulties in circulating the results to establishments as they conflicted with a commitment to the principles of IEP in Headquarters and a strong feeling expressed by staff that IEP had helped to put them back in control. The report was never published[13]. It was frustrating to witness remarkably similar difficulties with the operation of IEP in the much more volatile environment of the CSCs.

13. Copies were eventually made available to those who requested one.

6. IEP and the Close Supervision Centres

At the time of fieldwork for this project (May/June 1999), there were 28 prisoners in the CSC Units at Woodhill. Eight were on A wing (the restricted regime); seven were on B wing (the structured regime); nine were on C wing (the intervention unit) and four were on D wing (the segregation unit). A + D; and B + C seemed like two separate prisons ('control' and 'progression'). Staff reported confusion about their role on A and D ('Are we therapeutic or controlling?'). The 'stand-off' and 'control' orientation had arisen as a response to difficulties (of an unexpected degree) rather than as a planned feature of the CSC system. Staff had, despite clear signals in the Spurr Report that some prisoners would require long-term stays, expected to receive prisoners who were prepared to progress ('We thought we were going to get [named prisoner]s – people in a rut who wanted to get out'); and they had not expected the degree of psychiatric morbidity they encountered. Whatever the level of sophistication of the Spurr Report, a much simpler message had been communicated to staff about the purpose of the new system. Staff operated the new 'rewards and punishments' system to the letter in its earliest days, and this resulted in a violent and protracted negative reaction from prisoners:

> They just said to me you have got to sign a compact...every few days they would say to me, you've got to sign a compact, or you'll stay down here. So I said, well, I'll stay down here and this is where I've been ever since (prisoner).

There were tensions between prescriptive operating standards (*process*) and the handling of 'grey areas' (*outcomes*) as staff gained experience (eg. on B: 'Many of them don't come out on association. If we used the letter of the law, they should be off the wing. We have to manipulate the system to manage them. This way, they gradually come round'). Staff learned to be 'less confrontational' in their approach. Few prisoners had signed compacts on B wing; prisoners did not always clean when they were supposed to. ('They get to a level, they mix, and then we try to force them on further and that's when we get a problem'.)

B wing was a key location. Prisoners either succeeded or failed on this wing. Arrival on B wing often resulted in a substantial lowering of the level of material privileges prisoners had access to. Prisoners inevitably regarded this as punishment. Transfer from the former Hull CRC (which was the equivalent of Enhanced) to Woodhill B wing (Basic), for example, involved 'going back two places'. Material conditions in dispersal segregation units were often substantially better in practice than Woodhill B wing. Their direction of movement out of B (up or down) seemed to 'seal their fate' for the foreseeable future, with very different outcomes. There was a risk that once on A wing, the motivation to progress was lost, or replaced by the motivation to fight. Prisoners on A and D wings spoke of their immunity to material needs (and in one case, to suffering). They became determined to resist even those staff who went out of their way to talk them round. Prisoners used a language reminiscent of other segregation eras:

> You have feelings of just madness, feelings of real bad hatred, things you never even dream of (prisoner).

Some prisoners spoke of having expectations of help and 'treatment', but then discovering that the system seemed like 'just another form of control'. They complained that staff seemed unsure of what sort of help they needed.

Staff on B wing wanted to provide programmes and interventions for prisoners to encourage movement upwards. They wanted to become experts in the handling of extremely difficult (volatile, dangerous and sensitive) prisoners. The professional use of judgment by staff was critical to the operation of the system. But this was extremely difficult to achieve in practice.

As indicated in the CRC Report, there were always likely to be difficulties with a location-based scheme where particular wings (eg B) became unpopular because of the mix of prisoners, or the high numbers of prisoners awaiting assessment/transfer to psychiatric hospital ('They all know each other. They think it's full of fraggles'). There were also subcultural pressures on individual prisoners to resist (eg on A: 'you lose face, going up'; 'They've got their own criteria, and they have to fit that to survive'). There were problems with stigma and 'perverse incentives'.

As in the national IEP evaluation, it was difficult in practice for staff to separate restricted material privileges from harsh attitudes ('A and D are full of anger. It's a fight to the death'; 'How can you treat prisoners like that [on A and D], and then come on here [B and C] and want to be friends?'). When asked if it was the material level of privileges they objected to, prisoners found it hard to disentangle low levels of material provision from punishment:

> Int: So is it the material conditions they keep you in on B [that make you think it doesn't work?]

> P: No, it's more…yes, it is…people deserve more, they shouldn't come in here feeling punished, not able to have their own clothes (prisoner).

Int: Their argument on their side is that people will stay in units if they make it too comfortable, people won't want to recategorise down the grades, they'll want to stay here.

P: I don't think that's necessarily true. People only want to stay in these places if they've go something to hide from in the system...that's what I find, well, what I know.

I don't think this is the right way forward to handle difficult prisoners because it just embitters people, people just feel misjustified, in gaffs like A wing and D wing.. you see, it's down to restrictions...attitudes (prisoner).

Several prisoners detected a 'political agenda' behind this. On A and D, staff were beleaguered and had appeared to have a very strong (negative) culture. Prisoners responded with even stronger defences and bitter aggression:

Oh yeah, it's having an impact. I hate these people, whereas before I come here, I didn't have no trouble at all with no prisoner or staff (prisoner).

It don't mean nothing. And that's what they used to say to me, [name], how can you do that, you're coming out of your cell, you're whistling, you're singing, smiling, because they condition people. These segregation units, they condition people. Brutality, all it does is kill feelings. That's all it does. You know? (prisoner).

Several prisoners talked of the rage they experienced when they 'felt rejected in the way they were treating me'. One linked this to his damaged past:

What segregation done was actually brought back reminiscences of my childhood; very very sinister, very frustrated, very afraid, confused...like I needed to kill something, take it out on anything in his path.. (prisoner).

These 'unresolved histories' (see Bottomley, Liebling and Sparks 1994 on the Scottish equivalent) had to be addressed before prisoners were prepared to give staff a chance. Prisoners could not contemplate being 'subservient', but (often for reasons which made psychological sense) insisted on retaining some power, of some sort, of their own. This was their only available mode of survival (reminiscent of Cohen and Taylor 1972).

Relationships with staff then, were more important than, but were difficult to separate from material privileges. As in many penal settings, every staff action was symbolic and representative of the kind of authority used:

It does seem petty, a lot of the gripes of the prisoner to somebody on the street would seem really petty, but when you're...I mean for you to go into a cell and somebody slam the door, if you're not a prisoner, it's just somebody slamming the door, right? But if you're a prisoner and somebody slams the door, then it's a different, there's different connotations all round, you know what I mean? (prisoner).

As illustrated above, prisoners' judgment about the legitimacy or fairness of a regime was inextricably linked to their perceptions of their treatment (see further, Bottoms and Rose 1998; Sparks, Bottoms and Hay 1996). A and D wings were regarded as punitive, and staff exasperation added to a cycle of aggression, restriction, more aggression and more restriction:

It was expected that I would go down to A and D [by other prisoners]. But I am going in a different direction now... my time on B was not easy.. [talks about how all the momentum is to go down rather than up]. They give you a month and then they test you – it's too overpowering – you think you're getting punished. They put you in corners, pressure you all the time. You're trapped. I challenged the staff – it causes problems. I knew that if I went down there I would stay there. I'm not fighting, I'm trying to survive, with a bit of self-respect. There are two types of prisoners in here: those who stand up to the system and those with something wrong with their minds – they should be in hospital. They've got no vision here. There's no value in it [being here]. It's changed me [for the worse] being in here. I was having a war with these people. The whole place is bizarre. I think you hold it in [the fear and anxiety] but it comes out in different ways. You are at war, you're isolated; you get anxious just asking for exercise. It's like being interrogated – it's intense and extreme. It goes out of your control – you're compelled. This is about them making us do it on their terms. There have been loads of assaults on staff (prisoner).

Prisoners often mentioned the former CRC system, or the current dispersal system, as a place where they felt more respected and more in control of themselves.

One or two prisoners disputed their allocation, arguing that they did not fit the criteria, or that they had not been given adequate reasons for their move into the unit:

They say they put you here because you can't get on with people or you're violent. Whereas I don't fit that. I don't remotely fit the criteria. I might do now, but I didn't then (prisoner).

Prisoners also objected to the austere level of privileges they found when they arrived, something they linked to its operational philosophy:

I think the whole thing is designed as someone's plaything, someone who thinks that prisoners are going to jump through hoops whereas there is a lot of prisoners, there's about 12 or 14, who refuse to do the unit...I think I would have accepted it if they didn't try and take the radio and all that away. Because what happened, you come here and they take everything off you and that infuriated me (prisoner).

It ain't gonna work for the simple reason that as soon as you're down there, they're implementing the hate factor. Come here on reception and everything's taken off you. People, you're leaving segregation units and you come in here and you're being told, you're being led to believe something. You're told, when you go to Woodhill, we're going to try to do what we can to help you, you now, there's specialist staff there, they're equipped to deal with your problems, all sorts of bollocks, and you come here, and straight away they take everything off you (prisoner).

Staff seemed out of their depth, and had little support. On B and C, staff seemed more confident professionally and more satisfied in their work. All the wings were described as 'intense'. Some prisoners (especially on C) argued that they were motivated and willing to progress. ('At the end of the day, if you want to get out of here, you've got to work with these people'):

I thought, I've got two choices, I either sit down here and end up..'cause all that creates is desperate behaviour, me in a cell, got nothing to do, angry, feeling embittered against the system...I start brooding, chinning screws left, right and centre.. so I said to myself, just get through it, just get out of here... And I came through it. None of them believed I'd come through (prisoner).

There were feelings elsewhere in the prison that the CSCs drained the rest of Woodhill's regime (through staffing shortages).

Staff had insufficient training in a) the use of IEP and b) the handling of difficult prisoners. ('It's mainly guesswork. We sit round a table and say, what should we do next?'):

This is supposed to be a strict regime with no grey areas – but you need the grey areas. We have got the discretion to move them down, but not up. Staff are able and willing to do whatever we are supposed to do – but we don't know what we're supposed to be doing; and we don't have the time or the resources to do it. If we followed the operating standards, we would get nothing progressive happen. For example, if they don't come out on association, they should be off the wing. We manipulate the system, just to manage them. We think, he says he hears voices when he's banged up, so we don't bang him up. We operate with a complete lack of information – we know nothing about them; you see no specialists in here. This is more of a stand off. We had far more contact with them in CRC units. It was a much less violent environment. The big difference is it was voluntary. It was a much safer environment. You could spot things building up – a mood. Here, you just don't know what to expect every time you open a door. That's how it's developed. It wasn't intended – we were supposed to relate to them. But you can't [in these conditions]. This developed over time as we responded to their behaviour. We were told all this stuff would happen – we would have case conferences on each one before they arrived. That idea was just abandoned. (Officers – from notes)

Staff did not routinely receive information on prisoners prior to their arrival on a wing. As in other Basic regimes, no Psychology support for staff or prisoners was routinely available on A and D wings. (Arguably, this is where it is needed most.) In general, the seniority and level of experience of the psychologists working in the CSCs was surprisingly low, given the nature of the population. There was a lack of clarity and openness (in some cases) about the criteria for good and bad behaviour. ('Is showing willingness enough?'.) As in the IEP evaluation, more planning went into enhanced wings than 'at the control end'. There was some feeling among staff that 'progression' (eg from B to C) was automatic rather than the result of assessment. Staff felt under pressure to move prisoners up in order to demonstrate success ('Some are rushed through, for political reasons'). There was some competition between staff and prisoners to manage movements (eg should 'friends' move together?). Staff felt relatively powerless in the decision-making process.

There were 'privilege' inconsistencies between C wing (the Intervention Unit) and Durham. Not all prisoners saw a move to Durham or back in to the mainstream as 'progress'. There seemed to be a genuine tension between challenging prisoners' behaviour and managing it. Movement off a wing was not always the right 'tool'. In general, prisoners welcomed a relatively high degree of structure, but they also wished to be treated as individuals. Different interventions worked with different prisoners. Education was important in several cases and was identified as a key 'turning point' for some individual prisoners. There seemed to be a link between 'time left to serve' and improved behaviour: as prisoners reached the final stages of their sentence, they became motivated to progress.

Whatever the original intention, the structured regime was regarded as punitive by prisoners who were allocated to the CSCs. Many prisoners protested against the CSC system per se as they understood it – ie as a power struggle over the terms of long-term imprisonment or as an unfairly, and in some cases unexpectedly, limited special unit. The restricted regime was seen as worthy of bitter contempt. The material levels of privileges available were regarded as restricted even by those who designed the CSC system, within the constraints and context of the time:

> Remember in the midst of all this, Derek Lewis got sacked and Richard Tilt became Director General; Supermax was very much on the agenda; there were issues about golf courses for prisoners, disruption.. the context was very, very harsh in terms of the way that prisoners should be treated at that point. (Senior manager)

Staff interpretation of privilege entitlement was even tighter than the already tightly written Spurr Report intended, with prisoners unable to have pens on the restricted unit until an intervention remedied this.

Among the team involved in producing the Spurr Report, there was a reasonably sophisticated working knowledge of difficult prisoners. This flexibility of spirit did not seem to survive the superimposing of a simpler IEP framework for CSCs, in its transition into practice:

> With the structured system...I think, yes, but recognising that it cannot be very...you can't just say, 'this is the carrot, this is the stick, we'll hit you if you don't do it'. It's more complicated than that. You've got to be more sophisticated than that with these types of prisoners who play all sorts of games and who want to buck the system...you need individual case plans and assessments, and that was one of the things that was in there [in the Spurr Report], that the whole thing with these types of prisoners is you can't lay broad generalisations, you need to take each individual and work through a plan with them (Senior manager).

A Report of the Committee on the Prison Disciplinary System in 1985 (amongst others) had noted that:

> [I]f a more modern prison system is to be achieved, then emphasis must be placed on the carrot rather than the stick...The simple fact is that if prisoners have few privileges, they have little to lose (Home Office 1985).

In addition to the difficulties of convincing prisoners that their austere living conditions were justified, there was another major flaw in the application of IEP to this population. Both compliance and risk reduction were necessary for progression. This was confusing for prisoners who complied. For some prisoners, their compliant behaviour could not be rewarded in adherence to an earned privileges scheme if their risk remained unacceptably high. This was the cause of considerable consternation and protest. In this sense, of there being a distinction between compliant behaviour (over which it was assumed the prisoner had some control) and a reduction in risk posed (which might include behaviour seen as disordered or not within the prisoner's control), the 'carrot and stick' notion was an illusion. How to cater for the generally (or even sporadically) compliant but high risk prisoner became a major preoccupation of those staff who were held accountable for the delivery of the scheme to the most dangerous.

7.   Implementation of CSCs: from policy into practice

How did the CSC system come to look as it did, given the early experience with the Wakefield Control Unit, a national evaluation of IEP signalling the dangers of too stick-like a policy, and the amount of accumulated expertise in the management of difficult prisoners around at the time? Were there flaws in the Spurr Report or were there some important departures from the spirit and the letter of its recommendations in the implementation and early operation of the centres? As Paul Rock has argued, new policies originate in complex and often uncontrolled ways [14]:

Policy making is the instrument through which the original, subjective inspiration of a few individuals closeted within a bureaucracy can move out to become a public, anonymous, and objective component of the criminal justice system at large. It proceeds typically by preparing and submitting ideas to an ever greater mass of significant others for judgment and investment, and it turns, first, on the physical and symbolic incorporation of outsiders and secondly, on spinning webs of causality about itself and its projects. It is, in this sense, both its own object...and an object preferred to others for fostering. It would be an otherwise smooth metamorphosis were it not for the sudden lurches and opportunities imposed by uncontrolled problems of timing and context (Rock 1995: 16).

As is the case with any major report or inquiry (and arguably, with many policy instructions), the core concern (or gist) is digested and translated into activity – so that the Mountbatten Report was about 'security' and 'classification', the Radzinowicz Report was about 'a liberal regime within a secure perimeter', the Woolf Report was about 'delivering justice', and the Spurr Report was about 'progression'. None of these conceptions tells the whole story[15], and some important unintended consequences flow from these summary characterisations of official documents. The Spurr Report, which was never published, was interpreted (at least by staff working in the newly established centres) as a set of

---

14. Paul Rock also argued that the newest modes of policy-making have taken on a new form and speed, and require separate analysis. They are, he argues, 'the fruits of a new politics of populism, moralism, and the market' (p. 2).

15. These themes do represent the main concerns of each report. However, the Mountbatten Report endorsed 'humane liberal treatment aimed at rehabilitation' (p. 4), made recommendations about staff promotions, recognition and specialisms in security, training and rehabilitation and recommended improved administration. He also advocated extensive family contact and described his preferred regime as 'a liberal, and what might seem a permissive regime' which should be carefully introduced and controlled, with 'a few determined escapers prevented from taking advantage of it' (p. 88). The Radzinowicz Report did recommend 'a liberal regime within a secure perimeter', but the perimeter security envisaged was extreme and included some support (8 out of 17 Council members) for the presence of armed guards (p. vi).

recommendations aimed at moving intractable prisoners upwards and outwards, back to mainstream conditions. Its dual function was arguably underplayed, so that in its early stages more thought went into the progressive side of the system than into the regressive option, or the downward spiral. Arguably, many of the first prisoners to be selected were 'an easy selection' – prisoners who were at that time in dispersal prison segregation units but who had spent some time on ordinary location, showing some interest in conformity – chosen precisely because the indications were positive that successful progression might occur (personal communication). Other prisoners to be located in the CSC system in its earliest stages were selected from Hull CRC unit as it was strategically closed. The material contrast for prisoners moving into the structured regime from other locations was stark. The intended openness about reasons and procedures for allocation was slow to appear (R v Mehmet and O'Connor).

The first aspect of the Spurr Report which was not adhered to in practice was its broad notion of progression and the flexibility that would inevitably be required to achieve it. Whilst in terms of its *aims*, the centres became preoccupied with progression, in terms of its *practices* and *principles*, staff operated with a strict adherence to the rules (understandable in the wake of the Learmont Report, and in the light of the critique of the 'loose' CRC system explicit in the Spurr Report[16]) and the swift following of non-compliance with action, in other words, with regression. Within minutes of arrival, the first prisoners were downgraded from the structured to the restricted regime following non-signature of their compacts. Thus was to begin – at the hard end of the new CSC system – a destructive, systematic protest by its first inhabitants – a protest which generated judicial and ministerial interest, which devastated staff, and which led to 'control and restraint' lock-down conditions for a small group of prisoners for many months. Some of these prisoners became more violent (and more disturbed) than they had been at any stage during their prison careers. The number of prisoners ending up on the restricted regime, the degree of their intractability, the form of their protest and the length of time they remained, were unexpected.

Above the structured regime, on the Intervention Unit, a quieter life was formed, and several prisoners did succeed in leaving the unit and moving on to Hull (at first) or Durham and/or back to mainstream conditions, although even on this Unit (C wing), life was unpredictable. Staff succeeded in forming relationships with some prisoners, and some made serious efforts to leave behind their confrontational behaviour, and work their way back into ordinary locations.

---

16. Following the escapes from Whitemoor SSU and the highly critical Learmont Report, there arose a 'rule following backlash', supported by a belief that the integrity of any policy or system would erode as soon as any departure from stated practice occurred – privilege 'drift', appeasement and conditioning, and the risks of these, were the new terrors for the service. Some of the difficulties with this position are outlined elsewhere (Liebling, forthcoming).

The second aspect of the Spurr Report which did not survive implementation was the concept of the CSC system as in the instructions as a skeleton or *framework*, within which there was room for careful handling of individuals, and scope for *continual shaping of the system* as learning continued[17]. This was important for two reasons. The first was a simple recognition that learning would evolve, that accumulating expertise should be drawn on (in the Report, envisaged as a multi-disciplinary Committee) and that a blueprint could not exist. The second reason is more complex, and tells us something important about the policy making process. This was the problem of the dual purpose of any official report. Its first, explicit aim is to make recommendations for the handling of difficult prisoners: to address a difficult problem with carefully thought out proposals[18]. Its second is to fit the political climate and receive the blessing of Parliament:

> The difficulty in writing the report was that this had to all be sanctioned by ministers and the ministerial view at the time was very clearly in support of the very crude...Learmont recommendation that 'these people are bad, take everything away from them, make them earn something that's better'. And that was very much the political context and the debates we had about how we could actually [deliver]...there was a question mark at one point about what the entry level would be and whether we could get an entry level that wasn't going to be at basic level (Senior manager).

This raises key questions about what a policy is, and what has to be taken into account in order for implementation to be 'safe'. I have argued elsewhere (Liebling 2000) that a policy is a 'conception' – an idea based on 'the gist' of its contents, informed by the context in which it is implemented. Here, we see it is also a political instrument, with distinct audiences and a dual purpose. This means that in practice, the leap between how the policy reads (its gist) and what it is actually intended to achieve may need careful handling:

> What people did was take the skeleton of how it might work, which was partly about how do we get the system through the line and that became... the reality of this is the maximum allowed of everything...and there was scope to develop that regime as we gain experience and as we look to put the thing from the skeleton of a written report into reality.. (Senior manager).

17. Some learning did occur, but it was clearly negative. Some of this learning may account for the non-implementation of other parts of Spurr.

18. Even this apparently straightforward aim is complex – as the proposals designed to remedy one problem introduce new problems of their own. One major concern about the CRC system was the transition of prisoners back to mainstream prisons. There had been some very poor results, including 'when there have been ex-CRC prisoners who have murdered other prisoners when they've gone back onto normal location' (Senior manager). The solution to this difficulty became an over-rigid movement of prisoners through predetermined stages and locations before they were able to return to mainstream conditions. For some individuals, this seemed inappropriate and was dificult to justify. Again, the Report intended flexibility to remain in place.

An official report is something written to an often tight time scale (as Mountbatten and Radzinowicz both remarked in their reports), to fixed terms of reference, to produce a conception. The process of implementation requires considerably more 'shaping' of this core conception once the report is finished and its proposals accepted. This is most important in the translation and interpretation of a policy to the staff who implement it. Staff did not seem to receive clear messages about the complex task they were about to undertake. 'Progression', which is a complex idea in relation to this group of prisoners, was usurped by a simple notion of rewards and punishments (precisely the notion that the CRC Report had been at pains to avoid at all costs); and a tentative framework which required careful monitoring, support and adaptation was implemented as though simplified and (at first, in particular), that simple translation written in stone.

These two aspects of the Spurr Report – the confusion between its IEP framework and seeing the central goal as progression, and a view of the CSC system as a fixed model – were *conceptual* problems. A third, *operational* difficulty was in the preparation for and management of the CSCs, which fell far short of good practice and which left staff easily unsettled by prisoners. Opportunities for intensive preparation ('that crucial eighteen months') and high calibre management were lost, so that staff felt unsupported, under-led and unable to deal effectively with the extremely difficult behaviour they faced from the outset:

> Everything was in too much of a rush. Prisoner and staff expectations were too high (Senior manager).

There was no continuity between (or oversight from) those involved in writing the Spurr Report and the later team selected to implement its recommendations, so that its spirit was lost in the translation. Staff did not feel adequately led, either by their own management or by the host prison. Staff expressed much of their dissatisfaction in ways that prisoners could understand. The relationship between the Woodhill centres and the host prison was uncomfortable, as it 'sapped the rest of the prison' (personal communication).

A careful reading of the available material, from Mountbatten and Radzinowicz to Spurr, suggest that a more flexible system, with individual case management and some softened application of the IEP framework, was actually intended, at least by some of those involved in the creation of the new CSC system.

Conclusion: managing difficult prisoners in a new environment?

So, was IEP consistent with this new management strategy for difficult prisoners? In practice, IEP was seen as remarkably irrelevant to this group of prisoners by staff, and by the prisoners themselves. Nationally, there was evidence that its implementation had contributed, albeit falteringly, and along with many other policies introduced at the time, to higher levels of order in many high security prisons. There were procedural risks, with high levels of discretion given to staff and few safeguards surrounding its operation. At least one high security prison suffered a major disturbance on a wing where its implementation was perceived as procedurally unfair. Prisoners were placed on the basic regime with insufficient attempt made by staff along the way to cajole, persuade and through tactics of talk, convince prisoners that cooperation might be in their best interests. Without process safeguards, and some level of trust between staff and prisoners, the policy was angrily resisted. Just like the Spurr Report, the policy of incentives and earned privileges emerged and was implemented in a specific context. It was interpreted, for all sorts of reasons, as a 'mainly stick' rather than 'mainly carrot' policy. Its apparently simple message – 'prisoner behaves, prisoner gets extra phone card' – belied the complexity of behaviour and motivation and dovetailed with a popular but simplistic faith in the power of material punishment to secure compliance.

Whatever the merits it may or may not have had in the dispersal system, and in the prison system more generally, it had few merits in the CSC system, as implemented. The mingling of 'progression' with 'austerity', and the inevitable difficulties of keeping material and social or relational 'privileges' separate, made life at the sharp end of the new CSC system even more confrontational than its creators had anticipated. Two important but fine distinctions grasped by the IEP policy writers but rarely by its implementers were missed, both in its implementation nationally but perhaps especially in the early operation of the CSCs: the distinction between material and other goods and services, such as therapeutic work (the former distributed according to desert, the latter according to need), and the difference between taking away privileges and taking away respect. Staff distributed civility as well as material goods, whether they knew it or not. The perceived lack of legitimacy of its operation – from initial selection to the decision to downgrade and the lifestyle available on each wing, gave prisoners every excuse they needed to vent all the anger, frustration and hatred they could muster against its staff.

IEP depends upon a rational choice model of human behaviour – an instrumental reasoning which places material rewards and punishments at the centre of motivation. A rational choice model, especially on its own, is not appropriate for a group of emotionally unstable and often brutalised individuals, with very little control over their own behaviour and considerable experience of, and therefore habituation to, material deprivation. Perhaps counter-intuitively, a moral scheme may actually carry more weight. For some of these prisoners, their emotional volatility is inextricably linked to perceptions of fair or unfair treatment, and to their perceptions of respect. These perceptions are mediated (as we might expect) via personal encounters with staff. In these circumstances, any whiff of punitive sentiment is enough to reinforce a cognitive scheme that defines authorities as cruel and unfair, and their own position as wronged heroes for whom everything is experienced as punitive (and therefore counter-effective). The only way to separate the concept of 'strictness' from the concept of 'punishment' is to build in a legitimate material threshold (as Woolf argued, and as Tyler empirically established), to operate in a procedurally fair manner and for staff to retain a neutral and decent interactive approach, however difficult this might be in these environments. One small unit (Shotts) achieved something approaching this for a part of its history (see Bottomley, Liebling and Sparks 1994). It is a different model, based on therapeutic principles, and a belief that emotional containment – or always keeping the dialogue going – is more important and effective than material strictness.

The unintended direction taken by the CSCs was linked to a blindness to its essentially dual function at the outset: any chance of successful operation was lost when its IEP framework, and the climate in which it was conceived, convinced its staff that progression was the key and only goal, and that this goal would be achievable in a 'carrot and stick' manner:

> It was never intended to be a lockdown. There was always meant to be a door open (Senior manager).

The most important fine distinction that was never fully grasped concerned the notions of strictness and punitiveness. Relative deprivation, a hostile staff orientation (however gradual and 'well deserved') and a climate of austerity make this distinction impossible to bring off. Some high security prisons have managed the post-1995 'return to power for staff' and the scaling back of prisoner conditions of living in ways that prisoners have perceived as (only just) tolerable. The penal climate has explicitly become deeper, heavier, and more punitive (see Downes 1988; King and McDermott 1995 for their use of these terms). The strengths of what went before were the efforts made to work flexibly and patiently with individuals, and if not, to contain them humanely and hope for some change. That capacity to contain humanely and safely, and almost abandon simple notions of progression or 'treatment' – whilst keeping a door open – may after all be the cornerstone of a legitimate regime.

> The problem is not being too ambitious or impatient, without giving up (Senior manager).

References

Advisory Council on the Penal System (1968) *The regime for long-term prisoners in conditions of maximum security.* London: HMSO (The Radzinowicz Report).

Ahmad, S. (1996) *Fairness in Prisons,* University of Cambridge Ph.D. thesis.

Bottomley, A K; Liebling, A and Sparks, R (1994) *An Evaluation of Barlinnie and Shotts Units.* Scottish Prison Service Occasional Papers No 7: SPS.

Bottomley, K; Jepson, N; Elliott, K; Coid, J (1994) *Managing Difficult Prisoners: The Lincoln and Hull Special Units.* London: Home Office.

Bottomley, K (1995) CRC *Special Units: A General Assessment.* London: Home Office.

Bottoms, A E (1992) The Control of Long-Term Prisoners in England: Beyond the Control Review Committee, in K Bottomley and W Hay *Special Units For Difficult Prisoners.* Hull: University of Hull.

Bottoms, A E. (1994) 'The Philosophy and Politics of Punishment and Sentencing' in R Morgan and C M V Clarkson *The Politics of Sentencing Reform,* 17–49. Oxford: Clarendon Press.

Bottoms, A E and Rose, G (1998) 'The importance of staff-prisoner relationships: results from a study in three male prisons', in Price D and Liebling A (1998) *Staff-Prisoner Relationships: A Review of the Literature,* unpublished report submitted to the Prison Service.

Bottoms, A E and Light, R (1987) *Problems of Long-Term Imprisonment.* Aldershot: Gower.

Cohen, S and Taylor, L (1972) *Psychological Survival: the experience of long-term imprisonment.* Harmondsworth: Penguin.

Coid, J (1991) 'Psychiatric Profiles of Difficult/Disruptive Prisoners', in K Bottomley and W Hay Special Units For Difficult Prisoners. Hull: University of Hull; pp. 44–71.

Coid, J (1998) 'The Management of Dangerous Psychopaths in Prison', in T Millon, E Simonsen, M Birket-Smith and R D Davis *Psychopathy, Antisocial, Criminal and Violent Behaviour.* New York: Guildford Press.

Cooke, D (1989) Containing Violent Prisoners: an analysis of the Barlinnie Special Unit. *British Journal of Criminology* 29: 129–143.

Downes, D (1988) *Contrasts in Tolerance: Post-War Penal Policy in the Netherlands and England and Wales.* Oxford: Oxford University Press.

Home Office (1966) *Report of the Inquiry into Prison Escapes and Security,* (Mountbatten Report). London: HMSO, Cmnd 3175.

Home Office (1979) *Committee of Inquiry into U K Prison Services* (May Committee), London: HMSO, Cmnd 7673.

Home Office (1984) *Managing the Long-term Prison System: The Report of the Control Review Committee.* London: Home Office.

Home Office (1985) *Report of the Committee on the Prison Disciplinary System,* London: HMSO, Cmnd. 9920.

Home Office (1987) *Special Units for Long-term Prisoners: Regimes, Management and Research,* Report of the Research and Advisory Group on the Long-Term Prison System. London: HMSO.

Home Office (1991) *Prison Disturbances 1990.* (The Woolf Report). London: HMSO.

Home Office (1994) *Report of the Enquiry into the Escape of Six Prisoners from the Special Security Unit at Whitemoor Prison* (The Woodcock Report). London: HMSO.

Home Office (1995) *Review of Prison Service Security in England and Wales and the Escape from Parkhurst Prison on Tuesday 3rd January 1995* (The Learmont Report). London: HMSO.

King, R (1999) The Rise and Rise of Supermax: An American Solution in Search of a Problem? *Punishment and Society: The International Journal of Penology* 1(2): 163–186.

King, R and McDermott, K (1995) *The State of Our Prisons*. Oxford: Clarenden Press.

Liebling, A (2000 forthcoming) Prison Officers, Policing and The Use of Discretion. *Theoretical Criminology* 4(3): 351–375.

Liebling, A (1999) Doing Research in Prison: Breaking the Silence. *Theoretical Criminology* 3(2): 147–173.

Liebling, A; Muir, G; Rose, G et al. (1997) *An Evaluation of Incentives and Earned Privileges: Final Report to the Prison Service.* Cambridge: Institute of Criminology.

Liebling, A; Muir, G; Rose, G and Bottoms, A E (1999) Research Findings No. 87: *Incentives and Earned Privileges in Prison.* Research and Statistics Directorate: London.

Liebling, A and Price, D (1998) Staff-Prisoner Relationships: A Summary of Research. *Prison Service Journal* No. 120: 3–6.

Liebling, A and Price, D (1999) *An Exploration of Staff-Prisoner Relationships at HMP Whitemoor.* Prison Service Research Report No.6.

McConville, S (1996) *Special Units For Disruptive and Difficult Prisoners: A Review of the Literature.* Unpublished study.

Price, D and Liebling, A (1998) *Staff-Prisoner Relationships: A Review of the Literature.* Unpublished manuscript submitted to the Prison Service.

Prison Service (1996) *Management of Disruptive Prisoners: CRC Review Project Final Report* (The Spurr Report). Unpublished Report.

Rock, P (1995) The Opening Stages of Criminal Justice Policy Making. *British Journal of Criminology* 35(1): 1–16.

Scottish Prison Service (1990) *Opportunity and Responsibility: Developing New Approaches to the Management of the Long Term Prison System in Scotland.* Edinburgh: Scottish Office.

Sparks, R; Bottoms, A E and Hay, W (1996) *Prisons and the Problem of Order.* Oxford: Clarendon Press.

Toch, H and Adams, K (1989) Coping and Maladaptation in Prison.

Tyler, T R (1990) *Why People Obey the Law*. London: Yale University Press.

Williams, M and Longley, D (1987) Identifying Control-Problem Prisoners in Dispersal Prisons, in A E Bottoms and R Light *Problems of Long Term Imprisonment*. Aldershot: Gower.

Appendix 2   The special handling of difficult prisoners in comparative context: a note on research resources and research needs.

Richard Sparks (Keele University)

The aims of this short supplementary note are confined to:

i)   identifying some existing comparative sources of knowledge about and reflection upon provisions for the special handling of convicted prisoners whose institutional behaviour is considered so risky, disruptive or disordered by the prison system in question that designated provision must be made to isolate or seclude them and/or address their specific problems and needs; and

ii)   specifying certain needs for a) the more systematic collation and review of such existing knowledge, b) the generation of new data and c) further efforts towards conceptual clarification, with the aim of informing enlightened policy deliberation.

The limitations of this exercise should thus be made clear at the outset. For example, I do not claim here to offer a detailed or substantive overview of existing knowledge; rather I argue the need for such a review. Neither do I claim that the state of current knowledge is sufficient to provide decisive guidance to the present task of evaluating and reviewing the Prison Service's experiences to date in relation to the CSC sub-system. At most I suggest that proper awareness of the scope and limitations of existing historical and comparative knowledge can assist in contextualizing and clarifying the nature of the challenges and dilemmas that arise and perhaps in minimizing the risk of avoidable errors, especially those which involve the repetition or re-running of history.

1.   Introduction: on penal politics and the 'repetition compulsion'

It has become more or less conventional to begin reviews of 'special handling' problems by asserting that these stand amongst the most difficult and intractable that any prison system has to confront. Both McConville (1995) and H.M. Chief Inspector's thematic review of CSCs (1999) open in this way. Whilst uncontentious in themselves such assertions also beg certain questions. For example, if such problems are indeed approximately similar across the prison systems of all developed countries why is there such a paucity of agreed knowledge or practice wisdom about how best to deal with them? Or again, if such problems have existed since a quite early point in the development of modern prison systems (as might be supposed) why is the knowledge and experience gained in dealing with them not more cumulative and progressively refined (than appears to be the case)? Such questions are in fact of considerable practical import. They go to the issues of how social research and accumulated experience can be harnessed to inform policy. Can such policy be, in the current idiom, 'evidence led'? Why has it not always been so in the past? Is it just that, being intractably difficult, these problems are ones that each prison system must confront recurrently, alone, and in an ad hoc and improvisatory manner?

Roy King, in his recent discussion of the drift towards 'supermax' custody in the United States, puts the matter more cannily: 'It is safe to assume that all prison systems will find some of their prisoners much more difficult to manage than others' (1999: 182). King's point is that there exists considerable latitude for variation in how far different penal systems generate behaviour that they find unmanageable in 'normal' regimes and for discretion in how they opt to define and confront it. King's account suggests that the vagaries of political and penological fashion can lead, as in the USA in recent times, to an inflation of problem classifications (a kind of internal 'net widening') and to a preference for draconian interventions in response to them.

Even if we take it as given that (notwithstanding isolated examples of good practice or institutional design (King 1991)) the contemporary United States does not provide a model that we wish to buy wholesale, King's argument raises some general issues. For example, under what surrounding conditions are decisions to institute, expand or indeed close 'special handling' sub-systems actually taken? What motivational assumptions, resource constraints and political sensitivities attend those decisions? What, for the decision-makers, counts as a relevant term of comparison whether positive or negative in nature, contemporary or historical in origin?

Herein perhaps lie some clues to the problems posed above about the limited applications of (or limited uses made of) prior and comparative knowledge in this field. Decisions about special handling measures are, more or less by definition, not taken in placid or politically uncontentious circumstances. They arise when problems appear to be reaching a critical point; when previous arrangements seem to have become ethically unacceptable, legally problematic or practically unsustainable; and often, by extension, at moments of political and/or intellectual instability. They often therefore also involve a repudiation of the immediate past (as too permissive/too oppressive; too expansive/too limited in scope; as being based on an outmoded penological model and so on). Certain recurrent dilemmas arise, but knowledge relevant to their resolution may be lost or not sought out. The history of special units for difficult prisoners in England and Wales and Scotland is, I suggest, by no means short of examples of this kind of oscillation; and the under-utilization of the record of experiences that they contain looks at times like the result of a classic 'rhetoric of reaction'. Thus, despite more than 20 years of varied experiences the Barlinnie Special Unit is nothing but an over-indulgent flop. The CRC units risk becoming nothing but a cumbersome, under-used and 'unstructured' failure.

The converse danger to this repudiation of the past is its unknowing repetition. Thus, the levels of material deprivation, inmate protest and structural blockage lately experienced in the lower levels of the Woodhill CSCs stand meaningful comparison with experiences at Wakefield (in the 1970s) and at Peterhead and Inverness (in the 1970s and 1980s), and some of them might have been, in light of those experiences, foreseeable.

2.   Resources

It follows from my argument so far that I regard the knowledge resources that might inform historical and comparative understanding of special handling issues as being somewhat scattered, variable in kind and quality, under-utilized, largely untheorized and (at least so far as genuine cross-national research is concerned) embryonic at best. Here I undertake a preliminary typology of relevant materials:

i)   cross-national, comparative materials
a) The United States. Historically the main comparator employed in UK penal policy deliberation has been the United States. At least for the middle decades of the last century that country sustained a rich and conceptually challenging record of intellectual engagement with its prisons (much of this material is digested in Sparks et al. 1996,

chapter 2). However in latter years the tradition of American prison sociology has declined (Simon 2000; King 1999), and prisons literature has tended to bifurcate between a purely professional one and an (in my view defensibly) oppositional and polemical one (Parenti 1999; Wacquant 1999), neither of them strongly grounded in observational research. The experience (for better or worse) of prisons such as Marion, Florence or Leavenworth have an obvious claim on our attention, but it seems ironically indicative of both the level of current restrictions on research access and the underdetermination of policy by research that much of the most substantial recent work on control practices has been undertaken by a British scholar (King 1999). Nevertheless a limited amount of relevant material continues to appear (eg Useem and Reisig 1999). McConville (1995) also summarizes some developmental themes but presents no new empirical material. The only really active tradition of US scholarship meriting our attention (outside the purely psychiatric literature which exceeds my competence here) is that concerned with the impact of judicial decisions on the constitutionality of prison conditions (eg Feeley and Rubin 1998).

b) Europe. This last characteristic of American work (namely its interest in external oversight and judicial intervention) is one shared by the majority of work so far appearing on European comparisons of special handling issues. The major preoccupation here is ECHR convention-compliance, and the major producers of such material are the Council of Europe (especially through the Committee for the Prevention of Torture (CPT)) and member governments responding to CPT reports. This literature is therefore primarily inspectorial/legalistic in character and, however important, makes little or no reference to regimes, aims, or staff-prisoner relational dynamics outside the context of inspection visits. Vagg's (1995) review draws largely upon material generated in these fora and thus has a somewhat secondary, if not tertiary, character. Even so, some potentially intriguing research issues arise (such as the apparently greater acceptance of solitary confinement in Scandinavia than elsewhere in Europe). The most valuable discussion to date of the impact of the CPT on prison practice is that by Evans and Morgan (1998: 307–15 and appendix 7). These matters are of the liveliest interest to current UK policy discussion in light of prisoner litigation and the advent of the Human Rights Act. Nevertheless it remains to the best of my knowledge the case that no original cross-national, collaborative empirical European research has yet been attempted on systems, regimes, relationships and outcomes of special handling measures.

ii)   Intra-UK comparative and historical materials

For the moment it appears to remain the case that the most abundant (and perhaps most thoroughly researched) record of 'cases' of special handling experiments are those originating within the UK itself. The materials here are of course more familiar and I make no attempt at a comprehensive survey. My point is rather confined to arguing for the use of these resources in a properly comparative and historical spirit.

The range of materials that constitute the historical and documentary record of UK attempts at addressing problematic prison behaviour is diverse and calls for some attempt at synthesis. It includes: inspection reports in England, Scotland and Northern Ireland; domestic and European court rulings; parliamentary answers, ministerial statements and ministerial correspondence; circular instructions, standing orders and operating standards; committees of inquiry of the Home Office, Scottish Office and NIO – eg from Mountbatten by way of Radzinowicz, CRC, RAG to current discussion around CSCs in the case of England and Wales, and from the working group preparatory to the establishment of the Barlinnie unit to the establishment of the present system in the case of Scotland. Despite some exchanges of personnel at both practitioner and researcher levels (eg Bottomley et al. 1994) there has been remarkably little systematic comparative work on the English and Scottish cases (but see King 1994). Almost all of the academic research has been, unsurprisingly, expressly evaluative in character and tied more or less closely to one or other already-ongoing review process (see Sparks et al. 1996, chapter 1) and almost none of it has been expressly comparative as between the different UK jurisdictions. The intersections and exchange of populations between the prison and mental health systems remain abiding issues. Finally, there is the well-known but under-analysed written record of prisoner autobiographies, most famously those produced by Barlinnie SU inmates.

3.   Research needs

i) There is a strong case for more systematic and synoptic overviews of experience in the special handling of difficult prisoners both as between the United States and United Kingdom and between the United Kingdom and other western European countries.

ii) There is in particular a strong case for new data generation on current instances of such practice, involving a collaborative research effort and using a range of observational and documentary methods. Such research might have regard to, inter alia, selection processes; the size and locations of units (including security/design issues); the coherence/progressiveness of special handling sub-systems (and their integration with the prison 'mainstream'); experiences of legal challenge and political controversy; threshold qualities of life and other regime characteristics; motivational assumptions, incentive systems and entitlements (including 'less eligibility' and 'perverse incentive' dilemmas); the use of specialist staff and clinicians and interactions with mental health systems; monitoring, accountability and external oversight; staff training and morale and other management questions. Merely continuing to collate Council of Europe documentation will only ever illuminate a fraction of these questions (and leads to a conflation between inspection and research).

iii) Even in the absence of such new programmatic work there is a case for a more dispassionate and complete account than currently exists of intra-UK historical and comparative questions (especially on the points of similarity and divergence between the English and Scottish experiences).

iv) There is a need for new conceptual work to bring our understanding of special/small regimes into closer dialogue with the best available current work on order maintenance and social relations in prison settings.

Of the above i), iii) and iv) might all be accommodated by commissioning a full-length literature survey (perhaps supplemented by some fact-finding/archive-hunting visits) on a scale comparable to Ditchfield's (1990) general overview of control issues but with a special brief to digest theory and evidence on special handling issues. Point ii) evidently calls for a new substantive research effort of a kind not previously undertaken. It would be necessary in the first instance to investigate whether the research capacity exists to mount such a programme involving several comparator countries. I suspect it does. A constructive first step would be to convene a symposium or short series of symposia amongst European and or US/European researchers and practitioners in order to explore research resources and funding issues.

References

Bottomley, A K, Liebling, A and Sparks, R. (1994) *The Barlinnie Special Unit and Shotts Unit* Edinburgh: Scottish Prison Service.

Ditchfield, J (1990) *Control in Prisons* (HORS 118). London: HMSO.

Evans, M and Morgan, R (1998) *Preventing Torture: a Study of the European Convention for the Prevention of Torture and Inhuman or Degrading Treatment or Punishmet.*, Oxford: Oxford University Press.

Feeley, M and Rubin, E (1998) *Judicial Policy Making and the Modern State: How the Courts Reformed America's Prisons.* Cambridge: Cambridge University Press.

H M Chief Inspector of Prisons (1999) *Thematic Inspection of Close Supervisions Centres (August–September 1999).* London: H M Inspectorate of Prisons.

King, R D (1991) 'Maximum security confinement in Britain and the USA: a comparison between Gartree and Oak Park Heights'. *British Journal of Criminology,* 31.

King, R D (1994) 'Order, disorder and regimes in the prison services of England and Wales and Scotland', in E Player and M Jenkins (eds) *Prisons After Woolf.* London: Routledge.

King, R D (1999) 'The rise and rise of supermax: an American solution in search of a problem?'. *Punishment and Society,* 1: 163–186.

McConville, S (1985) 'Special units for disruptive and difficult prisoners: a review of the literature and principal issues'. Unpublished report to Home Office.

Parenti, C. (1999) *Lockdown America: Police and Prisons in the Age of Crisis.* London and New York: Verso.

Simon, J (2000) 'The "society of captives" in the era of hyper-incarceration'. *Theoretical Criminology,* 4: 285–308.

Sparks, J R, Bottoms, A E and Hay, W (1996) *Prisons and the Problem of Order.* Oxford: Oxford University Press.

Useem, B and Reisig, M (1999) `Collective action in prisons: protests, disturbances and riots'. *Criminology*, 37: 735–760

Vagg, J (1995) `*The management of disruptive prisoners – a literature review of European practices'*, Loughborough Consultants Limited. Unpublished report to Home Office.

Wacquant, L (1999) *Les Prisons de la Misere.* Paris: Editions Raisons d'Agir.

RDS Publications

Requests for Publications

Copies of our publications and a list of those currently available may be obtained from:

> Home Office
> Research, Development and Statistics Directorate
> Communications Development Unit
> Room 201, Home Office
> 50 Queen Anne's Gate
> London SW1H 9AT
> Telephone: 020 7273 2084 (answerphone outside of office hours)
> Facsimile: 020 7222 0211
> E-mail: publications.rds@homeoffice.gsi.gov.uk

alternatively

why not visit the RDS website at
> Internet: http://www.homeoffice.gov.uk/rds/index.html

where many of our publications are available to be read on screen or downloaded for printing.